The Secrets of Christianity

Publishing Rights Reserved © 2021 by Mark Vedder. In other words do not publish it. Copy it all you want if you can manage that without altering the text. Plus it is polite to credit this work.

Library of Congress Control Number: 2021906254
Vedder, Mark 1965–2102
    The Secrets of Christianity / Mark Vedder
    201 pp.
    Published in Mechanicsburg, Pennsylvania
ISBN 978-1-941776-54-4

2021
ISBN 978-1-941776-54-4
Publishing rights reserved
by
Mark Vedder
sufferingduckman@gmail.com

INDEX

The Secrets of Christianity.. 1
    spirit.. 3
    God wants us to want.. 6
    the Spirit of Christ.. 9
    liberty... 10
    Language of Soul and what Christ did with it... 12
    Growth does not mean us getting less evil........ 13
    our relationship with Creation............................ 15
    the Spirit.. 19
    God is everyone's God, not just the Christians.. 23

To the Christians.. 27

The Story in the Book of Hebrews................................... 40
    Part I   1:1—3:6 Introduction............................. 44
    Part II   3:7—4:13
                The Pool of Siloam: Apostleship.............. 57
    Part III The Great High Priest
      Section I 4:13—8:13 Melchizedek and the Law.... 74
      Section II 9:1—10:18 The Eternal Covenant........ 91
    Part IV 10:19—End Who is Coming Along
              and Where Are We Going?........................ 101

The Content in James.. 128

Paul's Mystery.. 171

Afterword.. 197

Introduction

This here's Burt. I been asked to write another interduction. What that means is I had to read a whole lot of stuff again. Can't say as I understood it; seems to be all about secrets and mysteries and whatnot. Dint see no ice cream mentioned anywheres.

But I kin say the part about God wantin' us to want was kinda neat. I always figgered there was something okay 'bout us likin' to do things. I like to do things. Just the other day I was tossin' Holly logs in a pile and I kinda worked up a sweat. Them logs is heavy. But I'll have some good chunks o' wood what to work with now.

That spirit stuff got real complicated real fast. I kinda skipped to the end where it mentions the body. I kin see my body but I can't see my spirit nohow. I figger yeah that stuff is there, but i still don't see it.

I liked that part about not cuttin' down so many trees. I cut trees down sometimes, but I kinda feel bad cause for the tree to be worth me cuttin' down, it's gotta be older than me. It's like I'm cuttin' down my grandpappy. I don't think he'd like that. But he's already passed, so you don't need to worry none about that. Anyways I liked that part.

Lesse, what else? Oh yeah, he writes a whole lotta stuff about the book of Hebrews. Hope I don't hafta read that again. I know there's folk what get real interested, but I just kept thinkin' about that hatchet that I mighta left out in the yard and whether I should go and check just in case I forgot it. I did go look after a spell, but it was already brung in. It's good to be sure though, I'd of hated to had have it got rusty.

That stuff about James was okay. Gonna hafta watch my tongue I guess.

Then there was that last part all about the mystery. Don't seem to me what people don't get about it. The way it sounds, don't no one get what's goin' on at all or not. Mebe what we needs is some better learnin. I got learned purty well back in the day, but don't know as I needed all that. Sometimes you just gotta put that chunk of stone where it goes and fergit about it like he says.

Course I'm kinda pleased I done read it all. He went and gave that last book what he wrote to his sister and after two months she says she got the first chapter all done. Now that's some slow reading. Mebe she still needs learned.

So there's my interdiction. This here book's not as short as that last one was. That's okay though, the rain was spittin' by the time I done finished it. Good thing I fetched that hatchet.

The Secrets of Christianity

It is about time for the torch to be passed from Christianity to what is next, just as Peter handed the torch of Judaism over to Paul for 'the times of the Gentiles' in his second epistle. One last hold-up is the fact that Christians, like the Jews before them, have neglected to look around and see what God provided for them in this most peculiar section of mankind's history. We are near the end of a journey during which we have been wearing blindfolds. A comparison of the issues with which the church fathers struggled and the issues of the last two hundred years demonstrates that while much of the promised land *has* been taken and enjoyed, a great deal more of it is still under the control of those who worship demons and sacrifice their children to Moloch, starting in the church.

The book of Hebrews opened a door which few entered, and the epistles of John still cannot be read far less understood while our self-centered teachings do not allow us to take the veil of unbelief off from our hearts. This is lack of belief in the goodness of God; that he is light and in him is no darkness at all. It is lack of knowledge of the Lord Jesus Christ in the full range of who he is as a man, and what man has become as the result of what he has done. It is lack of fellowship with the Spirit who has been relegated to a vague magical force instead of the source for our every action.

Before we can pass the torch to the new people that are waiting, we need an actual torch to pass along. Paul *did* write the things he wrote—whether we read them or not, John *did* tell us how to have fellowship with the Father and the Son, Jesus *did* say the things he said—whether we admit that he was addressing us or not, and Christ *will* present a perfectly prepared bride to himself

—whether we are part of her or not. The secrets of Christianity were not new but the living in them was. John tells this in so many words: No new commandment write I to you… again, a new commandment I write to you. The fathers of faith whose histories are in Genesis contemplated these things as hope. The companions of Christ that led up to Jesus worked toward these things through the Spirit of Christ which was in them. The writer of Hebrews presents these things to us by saying that *they* without *us* should not be made perfect. And here we are.

It might be useful for the coming generation to see the struggles of the last two thousand years for what they are rather how this world would like to paint them. This requires discarding history books as well as treatises on doctrine; they have largely been written by the god of this world of whom it is said ...but the God of peace will bruise Satan under your feet shortly. The divisions in Christianity must also be discarded along with much of the apologetics; it is all well and good to prove something, but first one must have some idea of what one is proving, and the demons already know that God is real and Jesus is in charge.

Here we will present several subjects in whatever form they take in the writing of them; God's word is living and makes its own choices as to how it is described; when we speak of matters that are larger than us, it is often best to allow the matters to present in their own manner.

The first subject is spirit. Next is that God wants us to want. Next is the spirit of Christ. Next is liberty. Next is the language of soul and what Christ did with it. Next is the fact that growth does not mean us getting less evil. Next is nature (creation) and our relationship to it. Next is the Spirit. And finally, God is everyone's God, not just the Christians.

spirit

God is spirit, and they that worship him must worship him in spirit and truth. The title of this section has 'spirit' without a capital letter because we are not talking about the Holy Spirit.

Second Corinthians three has not yet been understood by Christianity. It starts with a simple appeal to their request that he have a proper letter of introduction to visit them, he who had started and established their church. Then he goes into the attitude behind that kind of thinking, introducing the idea of the *letter* of something and the *spirit* of something.

He mentions that the veil of adhering to the *letter* is done away in Christ: "But whenever one turns to Lord, the veil is taken away." The next statement confuses everyone. "Now the Lord the spirit is." He *is* the spirit of things that allows us to have the freedom to act without worrying about whether we are following the *letter* of the old or new covenant. The new covenant is characterized by following the *spirit* of things rather than the *letter*. The Lord *is* this spirit. What does this mean? One practical effect is that he is going to judge according to *his* opinion as to whether we lived in the spirit of what has been given to us, not a mythical roster of how much we pleased God. Paul says "where the spirit of Lord, liberty there." James says, "So speak you, and so act, as those that are to be judged by law of liberty." This means that we are going to be *judged* by whether or not we walked in *liberty*, which can only be accomplished by appreciating the *spirit* of what God is saying.

What else does this mean? The 'kingdom of the heaven(s)' and the 'kingdom of God' are not on a schedule that can only understood by studying Daniel's prophecies and Revelation. The twelve legions of angels that were hovering to help Jesus when he was taken for crucifixion are still hovering. They were and are ready to bring in the 'kingdom of the heavens'. Jesus says, 'Let's give it 2000 or so years, and see what comes of following the *spirit* of what God wants first,' so that "to the principalities and authorities in the heavenlies might be made known through the church the all-various wisdom of God." We're not on a calendar of events, he's waiting for us and lots of other beings to 'get it'.

So what is this realm called 'spirit' which Jesus is in charge of? *Spirit* is about life. "He that is joined to the Lord is one spirit." We are "made alive in spirit." What does Jude say of the typical Christian? "These are those who isolate themselves; soulish, not having spirit." How did he know? The word of God can penetrate to the dividing of soul and spirit. Proverbs says that one who isolates himself seeks pleasure. "But God said to him, Fool, this night your soul will be required of you; and whose will be what you have prepared?" Under Moses' law we could not 'store up' obedience, it had to be fresh every day. Under Christ's law we cannot store up 'godliness', it has to be fresh every day.

Those of us who are "not in flesh, but in spirit" have not noticed that we are not in flesh, even though we are told so plainly. This requires having the 'Spirit of Christ' (working with him) and the spirit of Christ ('getting it') so that the 'Spirit of God' can live in us. Not in our flesh, for it lusts against *our* spirit, and vice versa. Our bodies become dead in the realm of spirit. This requires that the Spirit makes his home in us so that the body can be alive now. Before *the* Spirit can do this, *our* spirit needs woken up and vivified, at which point it realizes that it's in a body that is unconscious of spirit. So this being in a living body requires physical life power, and just as Jesus physically touched people to heal them, the Spirit makes his home in our physical bodies so that they serve more than the flesh *or* the soul; the resultant actions become real in the realm of spirit.

This kind of living, being led *to* spirit (Galatians) *by* the Spirit (Romans), from the first Adam, a living soul, to the last Adam, a vivifying spirit, filters down to the soul via patient endurance ("by your patient endurance gain your souls") to the end that the soul be 'saved' if we do not draw back or isolate ourselves. This is the *object* of us having faith, not the beginning of it; salvation starts with a new spirit; the soul takes a bit longer as both James and Peter point out. John adds the cherry on top in his last epistle by saying that it would be nice if this 'spirit', having made the soul prosper, could keep filtering down to the body itself… for health.

This is how eternal life in mortal bodies works. It is one of the secrets of Christianity.

God wants us to want

"Until now you have asked nothing in my name. Ask, and you will receive, that your joy may be full." These were some of the last words of Jesus. James says "You have not because you ask not," then, "You ask and receive not because you ask evilly, to consume it on your lusts."

Knowing what to ask for does not take a mysterious ability to know what things God approves of. It takes desire for life. The Psalm says "He asked life of you; you gave him length of days for ever and ever." Life goes forward. Using up life goes backwards. John says that all that is in the world—the lust of the flesh, the lust of the eyes, and the pride of life—is not of the Father but of the world. It uses life up. So James continues by saying "Do you not know that friendship with the world is enmity with God?"

When humans want to use life up for pride or pleasure, it is not true desire; it pits our spirit against our body and effectively prevents true desire. "For the flesh lusts against the spirit, and the spirit against the flesh: and these things are opposed one to the other, that you should not do those things which you desire."

True desire and true want is toward life. Paul desired to be with Christ because there is more life there. The woman wanted her daughter to live and Jesus said, "Woman, your faith is great. Be it to you as you desire."

Wanting to live and wanting others to live puts us in fellowship with God because that is what he wants. Wanting for pleasure or pride is a waste of our otherwise valuable ability to desire life. It also shows a lack of confidence. Humility is confidence; we can confidently accept the grace of God when we are not proud. With confidence we draw near to God. When we are near God, we want life. When we want life, we ask for it. When we ask for it, we get it.

Draw near unto God and he will draw near unto you. That is how we kindle desire. It is one of the things that God wants. It is also one of the secrets of Christianity.

the Spirit of Christ

"The Spirit of Christ is the fellowship of all those who, finding themselves alone, embrace the circumstances of their earthly journey; who together with him make perfect the accomplishments of Jesus Christ, who perfects all things." The Spirit of Christ has been working on earth since Adam. By the Spirit of Christ Noah preached to those whose spirits are now in prison. This was the Word of Hope before Jesus became man and made specific what that hope was to be. Yet the Spirit of Christ was able to offer every human this hope by the goodness of the gift given to every man: life.

This life is in creation and in God's word. Each alone are sufficient to give each man hope; together they are unstoppable except to those who indolently take from each as if they deserve it. These people make themselves suitable for destruction. This indolence existed before man, and the lake of fire was prepared for beings of this nature. Men, instead of learning from example, embrace this second death.

(When it says that the dead were preached to, it does not mean that Jesus while dead took a cruise across the River Styx and told everyone that 'Oh, too bad; here's the good news but you're already dead so never mind.' While quite silly, it is found in many creeds because people do not know how to read, and those that can read do not know the Spirit of Christ. It means that while they were alive they received the preaching of life through creation or the word; that though they are dead now they did not 'miss out' on hearing God's message. That having a much more complete and specific Gospel today does not mean that it did not exist previously.)

The Spirit of Christ is, was, and will be working in every individual who lives by faith. The Spirit of Christ is the individual fellowship of Jesus with each of his companions. It links us with all true humans regardless of time or place. It allows us to work together with people we have never met or heard of. It provided a clearing into which the Holy Spirit moved to unite the disciples of Jesus into one body; this clearing was the new specific faith in the new specific person that they shared.

The fellowship of the Spirit of Christ is forged by emotion, which is what the word 'suffering' literally means when Paul talks about "the fellowship of the sufferings" of Christ. It is the fellowship of the emotions of Christ. Doctrines, instructions, and teachings are not emotions. Thus the fellowship of the Spirit of Christ is open to the ignorant, the erring, and the untrained. And the emotional.

This is one of the secrets of Christianity.

liberty

"So speak you, and so act, as those that who are about to be judged by the Law of Liberty."

We mentioned this in the first section on spirit. It's in the third paragraph if you want to go back and read it. The law said what to do and what not to do. That's simple. Liberty does not say anything on the subject. That is not simple. To simplify Christian doctrine, teachers of Christianity turn Christianity into law. This is a good way to confuse everyone and has worked quite well: everyone is confused.

People ask the question 'Are we supposed to obey the ten commandments?' and get a garden variety of answers: 'Some of them', 'No, but it's good to do anyway', 'Yes, except for the one about the sabbath', etcetera. In some churches they even divide the law into ceremonial, civil, and moral; and have various ideas about how much we are to adhere to the law in each case. It seems to make a lot of sense except for the nagging fact that it is precisely the opposite of what scripture says.

James mentions that if we are going to do one single item in the law, we are obligated to do every single item in the law. All or nothing. Period. This means that if we're not going to kill because of commandment six, we also cannot wear clothing made of a blend because of Deuteronomy 22:11. All or nothing. While this is a very simple point, it leaves those who wish to make Christianity simple without their best simplifier: law. Do's and don't's.

John says "Sin is lawlessness." Oh. What law then are we under if we are not under the Old Testament law? That is plain from our first quote from James: the law of liberty. Break that and we sin. And there are two definitions of sin in the entire New Testament. Let's give them each a paragraph.

"Whatsoever is not of faith is sin." Deliciously simple. It's not what we do, it's whether we do it through faith. If we do a wonderful fantastic thing that helps many many people, and do it without faith, it is sin. That means doing it because we think we're supposed to or any other reason (such as improving ourselves) that distracts from faith, which is believing God.

"If one perceives the good and does it not, to him it is sin." Dangerously simple. Anything good we see to do that we fail to do is sin. This means no holding back and saying 'Well I don't know if I have enough faith to do that.' The faith is already inherent in seeing that it is a good thing to do.

The Law of Liberty is correspondingly simple. Christ says to us, 'You are free: do what you want.' Will we be judged on what we do? Yes, it says we must all appear before the judgment seat of Christ. What will we be judged on? One, on what we decided to do, whether it was of faith. Two, whether we did it or not when the faith was there to do it. This is excruciatingly simple. It is also one of the secrets of Christianity.

the Language of Soul
and what Christ did with it

There is a language shared by trees, birds, insects, horses, and humans. It is unknown to angels, computers, demons, or stars. It is the language of mortality; the language of soul. Beings with blood or sap inside who can die know this language. Beings who have passed through death remember this language, but no longer share it. It is the language of living mortals; the language of soul. In men it is found in the heart.

This is a unique language of praise relegated to the earth and its living inhabitants. "The heavens, the heavens, to Jehovah, but the earth has he given to the sons of Adam. The dead do not praise Jah, neither any going down into silence; but *we, we* bless Jah from now and to the age." And having just looked up the relevant scriptures, i have concluded that this is *not* one of the secrets of Christianity. It is unexplored in literature, and practical applications appear only in scattered anecdotal accounts with no distinctions made as to the vastly different realms of spirit and soul.

This is one of the secrets of the next age; may it flourish there. Let's move on.

Growth does not mean us getting less evil.

The transition that acceptance of the Gospel provides from a state of wanting to be reconciled with God to a state of confidence that we are reconciled with God puts the believer in a new and unfamiliar place: he now can grow.

Someone who has spent their life in a hole has spent a great portion of his life wondering what is outside the hole and considering ways to get out. Once out of the hole and on solid ground, his training in how to climb out of the hole are of little use. It is one thing to be free, but another matter entirely to learn how to use the freedom. As if this is not enough, every time we learn how to use a bit of freedom, it changes us. So the way to act free today is different from what it was yesterday, and a bit of consideration reveals the uncomfortable fact that learning how to operate today is not likely to tell us how to act tomorrow.

This is called growth. Growth occurs where there is life.

We can imagine the difficulty this scenario presents if we are a Christian teacher. Everyone wants us to tell them what to do and what not to do. That is not growth; in a tree, the twig of last year is the branch of this year. It is inappropriate for a twig to act like a branch or a branch to act like a twig. The Christian teacher must teach how to grow. I have 60 feet of Christian teaching on my shelves, and the collected words in all those books that teach how to grow would fit on this page. We may have missed something important.

Growth hurts but it is an exhilarating pain. Growth is always new, but always natural. Growth demands that we go to God afresh each day for brand new instructions that we have never heard before. Growth requires a relationship with God not as Savior, Father, Provider, Lord—all of which are also part of life—but as Creator. And not the conveniently distant Creator that we tuck into Genesis one, but the Creator who is actively creating us as we are thinking right now.

Does a child *improve* from age five to ten? Hopefully not. He learns, he grows, he matures; but the idea that a ten-year-old is *better* than a five year old is reprehensible. Notice how our minds do a slight hiccup when thinking about that last line. The idea that an adult is *better* than a child is reprehensible. "Unless you turn, and become as little children, you will *in no way* enter into the kingdom of the Heavens."

The idea that children are *bad* and learning to be *good* is rampant in most cultures. The idea that an experienced and honored elder is *better* than a young ignorant believer is rampant in Christianity. But scripture says we are transformed *from* glory *to* glory. One is the glory of the child or the acorn that holds the entire massive oak tree in its little shell. Another is the glory of Abraham who had accomplished all for God and ended his life in honor. Each is perfect before God in its place.

Growth has nothing to do with getting rid of sins; growth cannot even start until the issue of sin is resolved. God uses all the circumstances of our life—whether we are sinning or not—for growth. Nothing can interfere with the work of Creator. We can resist growth and be miserable, or we can embrace growth and have joy; either way he will see to it that we grow.

The 60 feet of Christian teaching on my shelf could, instead of saying 'Be good,' say 'Be new." But we do have the scriptures. And yes, this is one more of the secrets of Christianity.

our relationship with Creation

There is a parallel between creation and God's word. Even before John Darby's transformation of the 'rapture' from a bright hope to a get-out-of-jail-free-card as regards the tribulation and what may or may not happen in it, men were misappropriating their stewardship of the earth based loosely on the idea that God had placed them in charge of her.

If one stood up in a church and began ripping out pages of the bible to make whisky bottle labels and cigar wrappers, Christians would be horrified. But they think nothing of ripping out thousands of acres of untouched pristine forest and making whisky barrels and cigar boxes.

One can argue that there are plenty of trees and they regrow. Likewise one could argue that we have a surplus of bibles and the actual pages are just copies and we can easily print new ones. So why does the one scenario produce applause and the other horror? We will find that the parallel is not so disparate as just described. In both cases management is being violated.

There are two ways that management fails. The first is indolence. The workers are ignored, the vines allowed to suffocate the trees, the garden is unseeded. The second is greed. The coffer is scooped, the workers abused, the trees timbered, the garden paved. The difference between the manager of the earth (Adam and his kind) and the owner of the earth (that would be Creator) has been shown by the care taken by each. God cares when a single sparrow falls to the ground. Americans like you and me committed genocide on billions of passenger pigeons and shrugged.

As to indolence, the best forestry schools still do not know how to garden a forest. Why bother? ...let it grow back by itself. And pretend that the burning forests in California are unrelated. As to greed, if i want to visit a patch of woods that has never been timbered, it's a three hour drive. And i'm in the middle of a state named after those forests (Pennsylvania). And the air? And the water? And the soil? And the animals? Is there anything left of creation being managed at all? Who is making up the excuses needed for this destruction?

We don't have to go far to find out. How has the Word of God fared under human management? As to indolence, who reads it anymore? Christian self-help books or visits to a church on Sunday are so much easier. As to greed, how many of all the antichristian doctrines are built from piecemealing scripture to suit? The question was phrased with the answer already in it: all of them. Yes, all the doctrines.

Management has failed. One way to address this problem is to say, "Oh, too bad." Another way was vocalized by Jesus: "Because of this I say to you that the kingdom of God will be taken from you and will be given to a nation doing the fruits of her." Odd that he says 'nation' there. As in, 'Not the nation that you are in.' As in, 'Not the industrialized, civilized, or religious nations.' The ones with phones and bibles and cars. Who shoot buffalo and build dams just for the hell of it. Literally.

This is called *destruction* by scripture—both of Creation and the Word of God—and is unilaterally met by God with the destruction of those destroying. "Your wrath is come, and the time of the dead to be judged, ...and to destroy those that destroy the earth." "*I* testify to every one who hears the words of the prophecy of this book, If any one will add to these things,

God will add to him the plagues which are written in this book. And if any one take from the words of the book of this prophecy, God will take away his part from the tree of life, and out of the holy city, which are written in this book."

In the oldest book in our Bibles, after thirty-five chapters of discussion on issues that mankind still faces, God steps in to personally clear up the situation. To solve the questions of sin, righteousness, wisdom, and justification, God discusses one thing and thing only: his physical creation. How many people find this puzzling? Virtually everyone. We have out of hand dismissed one of God's greatest witnesses, which happens to include our own bodies.

As to creation, everything is sacred, but there to be used *provided it is managed with the wisdom that Creator provides*. Lions have never yet wiped out a species to satisfy their bellies. As to scripture, everything is sacred, but there to be used *provided it is managed with the wisdom that Provider gives*. Heretics tiptoe around certain doctrines to make sure that they don't blaspheme. The Buddhists tiptoe around stink bugs on the sidewalk. That is not care, that is exaggerated fake care to excuse not learning about how God cares. It's called idolatry because we make our management ideas more important than the Owner's.

When we leave a chapter of the bible that we have read, we leave it more vibrant and meaningful than when we approached it, even though we have taken a great deal from it. When we leave a forest we have managed, we leave it more vibrant and flourishing than when we approached it, even though we have taken a great deal from it. The word of God is alive and interacts with us; it is not merely something to be used for belief or doctrine. Creation is alive and interacts with us; it is not merely something to be used for resources or infrastructure.

Creation and the Word of God are inseparable. They are both perfect. Our relationship to creation is how our physical body operates in the physical world. Until the Owner puts us in charge of a different kind of body, he holds us accountable for both how we manage this body and the creation with which it coexists. This is one of the secrets of Christianity.

the Spirit

"But I say the truth to you, It is profitable for you that I go away; for if I do not go away, the Comforter will not come to you; but if I go I will send him to you. And *he*, coming, will convict the world: of sin, and of righteousness, and of judgment. Of sin indeed, because they do not believe unto me; and of righteousness, because I go unto the Father, and you see me no longer; and of judgment, because the prince of this, the world, has been judged." "But when that one comes, the Spirit of the Truth, he will guide you into all the truth: for he will not speak from himself; but what ever he hears he will speak; and he will declare to you what is coming. *He* will glorify me, for he will take of mine and will declare to you. All, whatever the Father has are mine; because of this I have said that he takes of mine and will declare to you."

This happened.

For the first time, humans not only had the Spirit of God come on them, but actually have him living in their heart. This means constant access to the comfort of the Holy Spirit, the communion of the Holy Spirit, the love of the Holy Spirit, and the unity of the Holy Spirit. He seals us, washes us in regeneration and renewal, sets us apart, justifies us, jumps in when we don't know how to pray, communicates his fellowship with us to Christ, and produces fruit in us.

So why don't we feel anything?

Because no measuring stick large enough exists for humans to use on the Spirit. We can not see him or feel him, only his effects. Like fruit. Or enlivening. Or joy. And because of the self induced confusion we use to protect ourselves from too much communion with God (or he might *get* us somehow), we do not practice seeing good effects. We excuse away good things when they happen, and call bad things good. In order to do this, we must judge the motivations of ourselves and others instead of the much easier practice of accepting good where we find it. If a psychopathic cannibal holds the door open for me, I don't have to imitate him and go out and eat people. All I have to do is walk through the door and say 'thank you'.

So what's the big deal? Just try to see the good in things?

Suppose we fix someone's car and they give all the credit to some incompetent person who just stood there and watched us fix it. Not only are we being slighted, but the next time the car needs fixed the owner will go to the incompetent person instead of us. Then the useless fellow will probably come to us for help to fix it while he takes the credit again. And tragically, we will often comply just so that the car gets fixed. This is not okay.

If we were an invisible being like the Holy Spirit and could only be perceived by the *effects* of what we do, it would be very important that these effects be recognized, or we might as well not exist.

The Holy Spirit is directly responsible for good effects. Is someone holds the door open for us knowing that the floor is wet and hoping that we will fall on our face, and God keeps us from falling on our face, it is still a good thing that he held the door open and we can still say 'thank you'. If our siblings sell us as a slave hoping to never see us again and we become ruler of the foreign land where we were sold, we can welcome our siblings to share our kingdom and all the good effects that came with them selling us. Joseph's brothers never got this. Evil intentions only affect the people with the evil intentions; not the one being evil intentioned. *He* learns patience; murmurers learn nothing.

If we get jealous because someone is doing something with good effects that we are unable to share, we will be tempted to attack their motivation and methods. And say the good isn't good. This is a good way to go to hell.

"Whoever will speak against the Holy Spirit, it will not be forgiven him, neither in this age nor in the coming."
"Whoever will speak injuriously against the Holy Spirit, to eternity has no forgiveness; but lies under the guilt of an everlasting sin."
"Whoever will say a word against the Son of man it will be forgiven him; but to him that speaks injuriously against the Holy Spirit it will not be forgiven."

We have a word for this practice in English: Gossip. Now consider: How much gossip occurs in Christian churches?

When the Holy Spirit is grieved and quenched we do not have access to the effects of what he does. If he cannot affect us, he will go to those whom he *can* affect; we have no control over what he does. If we drive him away by being jealous of those doing good that we do not share, think about how jealous we will be when psychopathic cannibals are touched by him and do good things that we cannot share. All the troubles and persecutions of the church that we read about in the New Testament were fomented by jealous Jews. Now it is jealous Christians.

Christ told us that he would spew Christianity out of his mouth.

When is this going to happen? Unfortunately we do not know because we have quenched the Spirit. "He will declare to you what is coming." We have stopped listening to him and have become experts in calling good 'evil', and evil 'good'. This prepares us well for the unpleasant surprise of good happening to people who are not us. Our response will be to persecute and condemn them so that the wrath of God can fall on us completely. This is the practical conclusion of ignoring the Holy Spirit.

The unique age of mankind in which the Holy Spirit himself lives in the physical hearts of humans wraps up with their rejection of him, and thus, the rejection of the Lord who sent him. The path through this is the fellowship of love, joy, peace, patience, kindness, goodness, faithfulness, meekness, and self-control. These allow us to pass from one age to the next without our jealous biases. It is one of the secrets of Christianity.

God is everyone's God, not just the Christians.

"And they are breaking off—the people—the pendants of gold that are in their ears, and they are bringing to Aaron, and he is taking from their hand, and he is forming Him with chisel, and he is making a molten calf. And they are saying, These, your gods, Israel, who brought you up from land of Egypt." This nice thing about this new god that Aaron made was that it was not the God who created the heavens and the earth, nor the God of Abraham, Isaac, and Jacob… it was *their* God. A personal special god—'gods' really—that brought them from Egypt. No need to worry if this calf cared about the trees or all mankind or even if he had his own ideas about their future. He was their personal god, and now they could have a big drunken naked party. Which they did.

Moses did not think much of this new personal god or the magical story about how he came about: "And I am saying to them, To whom? gold? break from yourself. And they are giving to me, and I am tossing into fire, and he comes out—the calf—even this!" Aaron missed the part about the enormous amount of work chiseling and casting a monstrosity large enough for several million people to party around.

Oddly, the depersonalization of God goes hand in hand with the personalization of him. It's now a special god who just cares about them, but has to be pluralized into 'gods' in case some people's personal needs are widely divergent from other personal needs. One person needs a god who admires how holy he is acting and his neighbor needs a god who will forgive his debauchery.

Does this 'personalization' of God appear in Christianity? Why is it that preachers preach that someone needs to accept Jesus Christ as their own *personal* savior? What does 'personal' have to do with it? Why does scripture never use this term? They might as well say, 'Here you go, your own personal calf.' Because one cannot very well have a *personal* creator of the heavens and the earth.

Moses put an end to that. He ground up the calf, spread the results on the water, and made the people drink it. 'You want personal, here you go: right into your personal bellies. Enjoy the diarrhea.' They did get these gods back after the kingdom split under Solomon's son, "And he consults—the king—and he makes two calves of gold, and he is saying to them, It is too much for you to go up to Jerusalem: Behold your gods, Israel, who brought you up from land of Egypt!"

When Paul preached the gospel on Arion-Pagon (Ares Hill) he not only introduced the Universal God who makes and supports everything, he stated specifically how this God treats the vastly differing people of the earth:

"The God that made the world and all in it, he being Lord of heaven and earth, lives not in temples made with hands; nor is it because he is lacking anything that he allows men to serve him. It is he who is giving to all life, and breath, and everything. And besides he makes out of one blood every nation of men to be living on every facet of the earth, <u>having determined beforehand the seasons and boundaries of where they live so that in seeking the Lord they might actually touch and find him</u>. And surely he exists not far from each of us, for in him we are living and moving, as also many of your poets express, for we are also his offspring."

He starts with creation. Then introduces life; all of it. Then the fact that every single nation on earth has a place set up by God to find him. Then the fact that this is what we would expect if we are his offspring. Then in the part not quoted above, goes on to introduce resurrection life, which is what the Gospel was sent to tell us about.

When is the last time *that* gospel has been preached? And if it isn't being preached, *why not?*

When we preach to the Bambuti tribe in the Congo rain forest, do we tell them about God or '*our God*'? Do we recognize and respect the "seasons and boundaries of where they live" or impose upon them ours? We build them schools and churches and hospitals so that they can be more like us. Because our gods have more gold than their gods.

Meanwhile, back where someone is actually talking about God, a message is given to us Christians: "There will be the weeping and the gnashing of teeth when you will see Abraham and Isaac and Jacob and all the prophets in the kingdom of God, but yourselves thrown out. And they will come from east and west and from north and south and will be settled in the kingdom of God. And perceive: there are last who will be first, and there are first who will be last."

Message to Christians: if you want your own personal god (gods actually), you can have him (them actually). But don't confuse these gods with the Creator of the Universe to whom every nation on earth belongs whether they know it or not.

There are those in Christianity who honor God. It is difficult because they must be allied—by being Christians—with those who make Christians gods. The Israelites who did not want to bow down to Aaron's calf could hardly go off and make their own Israel (though some denominations in Christianity do try to do that). They had to wait until Moses came down and got rid of it.

Meanwhile the fact that what most Christians are worshiping are gods of their own making remains a secret of Christianity.

To the Christians

1 And we know that if Jesus Christ be the same yesterday, today, and forever, that the all things abide in that sameness, especially his own. 2 For here we have no lasting city from the time that his own received him not. 3 Wherefore the Church, the house of God, is built to a temple, this temple being the New Jerusalem, 4 which also is the Bride, the wife of the Lamb, brought into being as the mother of us all before the foundations of the earth, but to be manifested shortly at the apex of the ages of the heavens. 5 Yet those in past times who have looked for such a city received not the promises, 6 for just as we partake of the root and fatness of the faith of the fathers as a wild branch grafted in, so also they hoped in a city in which tabernacled God himself, 7 which tabernacle are we if we keep the watch for the day of the Lord with faithfulness, willing to keep his word with patience and not as some expect, to grab our way into his kingdom, whose reward will be according to their works. 8 For we have been made stewards of his gifts, the believing and the unbelieving, that each might be manifest by his fruits.

9 This city, once the gathering of living stones, but then the living gathering, both composed and dwelt in by saints, us and them, is of eternal subsistence and origin. 10 Wherefore also it could not be made manifest until life and incorruptibility were brought to light; 11 for itself has no need of a temple, the Lord God Almighty and the Lamb dwelling therein. 12 Nor needs it the physical service of the sun or moon, for its foundations are precious stones, its streets transparent gold, and its lamp is the Lamb. 13 For the law was a shadow, Christianity an image, but this city abides eternal, unmoved while the earth and heavens pass away.

2 But finding we have to do with a mother of eternal origin, what says the scripture regarding eternity? 2 "For thus says the high and lofty one that inhabits eternity, and whose name is Holy; I live in the high and holy, and with him that is of a bruised and humble spirit (that is, the Christ) to revive the heart of the bruised ones. 3 For I will not always be angry; for the spirit would fail before me, and the breaths I have made." 4 And further, he says of this humble steward of his word, "For the iniquity of his covetousness was I angry, and smote him; 5 I hid me and was angry, and he went on backslidingly in the ways of his heart. I have seen his ways, and will heal him, and I will lead him, and restore comforts unto him, and to those of his that mourn. 6 I create the fruit of the lips: Peace, peace to him that is far off, and to him that is near, says Jehovah, and I will heal him. 7 But the wicked are like the troubled sea, which cannot rest, and whose waters cast up mire and dirt. There is no peace, says my God, to the wicked."

8 For the wicked are without the gate of this city. 9 For though the High One was angry with his covetousness (that is, the desire of Christ's heart) yet what God sees he acknowledges, 10 for he will not look upon sin. 11 So having looked upon and seen his ways, he heals, leads, and restores both him and his mourners. 12 For the ways of God are abundantly evident: He that inhabits eternity dwells with the humble; 13 for the Christ will put down all rule and authority and power that none stand between the Highest and most humble, that is, Jesus. 14 But before his ways were seen, it says, "For the iniquity of his covetousness was I angry, and smote him; I hid me, and was angry, and he went on backslidingly in the ways of his heart." 15 Yet we know that the Christ sinned not; but that the counsels of God be centered on him, the scripture, in pictures, clearly manifests the beauty of his heart. 16 Ignoring which, we find ourselves vaunting ourselves by our own morality (which is not our own, but the law's) against God. 17 For that which God is doing on the earth will touch every soul.

3 For God is exalted, and though he dwells with the humble, he himself is not humbled. 2 For the true humility is hard to be understood, thus it is impossible but that offenses do come. 3 So he says "Lift up the stumbling block from before my people" for he is not willing that any should perish. 4 Yet *he* says, "Those you gave me I have kept, and none of them is lost, but the son of perdition, that the scripture might be fulfilled." 5 But to them he says "All you will be offended because of me this night." 6 Yet into this night he speaks late, saying, "These things have I spoken that you should not be offended." 7 But the shepherd was smitten and the sheep were scattered, for God said "For the iniquity of his covetousness was I angry, and smote him; I hid me, and was angry." 8 For Jesus, in the proving of true humility, speaks of himself and offenses thus: "But woe to him through whom they come." 9 As is seen in Jeremiah, "Woe to me for my hurt; my wound is grievous, but I said, this is a grief, and I must bear it. 10 My tabernacle is spoiled and all my cords are broken; my children are gone from me and they are not." 11 But what of the stumbling block? For that he was lifted up from before his people, we see "The stone which the builders rejected, the same is made the head of the corner, and a stone of stumbling and a rock of offense." 12 But that the heavenly city might not have its origin on the earth he says, "And I, if I be lifted up from the earth, will draw all to me." 13 So in his lifting up he is a stone of stumbling and a rock of offense to those disobedient to the word, but to those who in humility hope in a city built by God, he has become the living corner stone. 14 For what did he gain by going on backslidingly in the way of his heart? 15 Forasmuch as it could not be seen as humility until its fruition, it brought a smiting from God, until these ways were seen of God.

4 For the word of God that he was sent to preach was not a word of humility, but of the kingdom of God, 2 which is established in power, and in judgment, and with the baptism of fire. 3 Thus speaking in the world he says "Jehovah, you have enticed me and I was enticed; you have laid hold of me, and have prevailed: 4 I am become a derision the whole day; every one mocks me. For as often as I speak, I cry out; I proclaim violence and spoil; 5 for the word of Jehovah is become to me a reproach and a derision all the day. 6 And I said, I will not make mention of him, nor speak any more in his name: 7 but it was in my heart, as a burning fire shut up in my bones; and I became wearied with holding in, and could not." 8 Then how could this word of God be spoken in humility? And who can bear the yoke of prophesying?

9 For there arose no prophet since in Israel like Moses, whom Jehovah had known face to face. 10 For the man Moses was very humble, above all that were upon the face of the earth. 11 Yet the anger of Jehovah was kindled against him, for he had said "Ah, Lord! I am not a man of words, neither heretofore nor since have you spoken to your servant, for I am heavy of mouth and of a slow tongue." 12 And the anger of Jehovah was kindled against Moses, and in this anger was Aaron given his place, 13 who before the people fashioned a golden calf from the rings of their ears, 14 giving over their adornment unto idolatry, and leaving no room for wisdom; 15 as it says in the Song of Jehovah, "Oh that they had been wise!" for he that is wise will hear.

16 For a priesthood, having been established through necessity and not by the promise of life, finds its application subject to a law of worldly elements 17 for to this priesthood even mercy was subjected till the time that God would rest his anger, having found a guarantor of the good pleasure of his will. 18 For the image of God was created by one and unto one, 19 but abiding in incompletion, remained apart until gathered into one man 20 who destroyed responsibility to this incompletion by subjecting a finished work to a death of shame.

5 For a true and humble heart, in simplicity and sincerity, would subject itself to God's anger for the sake of God first, then the people, and not his own. 2 For Moses says "Jehovah was angry with me on your account, and would not hear me, and Jehovah said to me, let it suffice you—speak no more unto me of this matter!" 3 And wisdom was justified by Moses' speaking before the people, 4 for Jehovah had said "Speak unto the rock," yet Moses spoke unto the people and smote the rock. 5 So he that had angered Jehovah by reluctance to speech angered him a second time by speaking, and this to the sons of Jacob from himself. 6 And God, finding none to hallow him, hallowed then himself in his people, and water came forth from the rock. 7 For this Moses saw that one who speaks God's word in mortality must needs come under that word himself, or be found a liar, 8 as befell the prophets before Ahab and Jehoshaphat. 9 But being in fellowship with wisdom, he placed himself in condemnation, 10 that Jehovah, having hallowed himself in his people apart from the priesthood, might not forsake his chosen when the priesthood failed. 11 But the humility of being made a curse for the people of God is not put to account until the transgression of the curse is healed. 12 For Jehovah said, "I will show mercy on whom I will show mercy," 13 and he who on the night of observance to Jehovah, led the people through the Red Sea on dry ground, looks upon the goodness of Jehovah, asking the Lord to go in their midst. 14 And by reply he says "Behold, I make a covenant: before all your people I will do marvels that have not been done in all the earth, nor in any nation: 15 and all the people, in the midst of which you are, will see the work of Jehovah; for a terrible thing it is that I will do to you." 16 And Moses becomes the law-giver, and blessed the children of Israel before his death, for he was king in Jeshurun. 17 Thus the servant of Jehovah, the greatest prophet until John, having desired blessing for God's people unto his own condemnation, 18 dies in the land of Moab without being given the desire of his heart to enter into the land.

19 And he buried him in the valley in the land of Moab, opposite Beth-Peor; and no one knows his sepulcher unto this day. 20 Thus humility, the place of fellowship of God Eternal, is found in giving over the desire of the mortal heart unto hope.

6 For God, having chosen the weaker vessel in which to complete his image, caused a deep sleep to fall on Man, and to this day he sleeps. 2 But we who were taken from this image ought not to be found sleeping, 3 for a bright and morning star has risen in our hearts and the day is already upon us; 4 it is imperative that we take courage, and clean ourselves, for the change of our clothing is drawn near, and the time has arrived to go up to the house of God. 5 For we are already in his presence, and the feast is set in order, 6 in which many last will be first, and many mockers, grown used to the forms of the night, and faithful only in preserving doctrine without faith, 7 will trouble themselves to find the door from the outer darkness, 8 for there is no place before God for indolence in the stewardship of his gift, eternal life.

9 But woman having been brought into the world, man falls silent. 10 For truth speaks from the youngest of a family, even as the sensitivity of hearing is found in the most delicate bones of the body. 11 And having hearkened to his wife, and embarked upon the backsliding of which Jehovah speaks, he calls her name Eve, for she is the mother of all living. 12 For it is by her travail in childbirth that the son of man will be born, who establishes the image of God in himself.

13 Consider then this woman, first of her kind, created last of all life, called mother of all living. 14 For in her fashioning hope is delivered to the entire creation, 15 and having taken her *from* man, God shows that faith, belonging *to* man, is of the substance *of* man. 16 For believing, not in ourselves as we find ourselves, but in God who is forming us as we speak, we find ourselves unto a new flesh which is begotten in hope, 17 by which we have

been subjected to the very vanity that impels us to look for that city which is mother of us all.

18 For Eve, having begotten Cain, looked for another in the place of Abel, whom Cain killed; 19 but Wisdom's delights are with the sons of men, and *all* her children rise up and call her blessed. 20 How much greater then is this woman Wisdom, who through Eve's pain in labor brings the fellowship of eternity to the Son of Man? 21 Of her it says, there is no object of desire equal to her, whose husband is known in the gate, whose own works praise her. 22 For hope makes not ashamed, and the heart of her husband confides in her.

23 But in Eve we see the confidence of Adam, that, though she were deceived, yet would he commit to her the subjection of the creature to vanity, 24 that hope would not be apart from the work laid on him by God regarding his pleasure. 25 For even as by her fashioning hope was delivered to the entire creation, so by her travail is secured the bringing forth of the son of man, 26 by whose life creation is secured, both this, and soon, the next. 27 For man must return to the ground from which he was taken, but the seed of the woman through hope was delivered out of death and abides for eternity. 28 For his glory is seen in the sun, but this hope has the glory of the moon, a city whose streets are transparent gold. 29 The gold in Solomon's temple covered the wood entirely, which wood covered the stone entirely, that gold only would be seen. 30 But these streets are pure gold, as transparent glass, and there night no longer exists. 31 For in this hope did all the prophets born of woman obtain testimony from God; and their works could not be contained by the old skins provided in statute and law; 32 wherefore he always provides of his Spirit, 33 that as his Son was in the world, so they and we would partake together in the building of the selfsame tower.

7 Now the Spirit of Christ is the covenant of fellowship, the enactment of prophecy; 2 for by this spirit we accompany the

Christ. 3 By the Spirit of Christ Adam ate of the fruit of the tree of the knowledge of good and evil, he being with his wife, and brought the earth over which he had been set into a conflict which demanded a new manner of involvement of God. 4 By the Spirit of Christ Abel became a shepherd, recognizing that he had been removed from the place that God had set Adam to till and guard. 5 And his brother, desiring to reestablish man's place over woman's (in that he brought the fruits of toil) found no satisfaction until he had destroyed the evidence of humility. 6 By the Spirit of Christ Lemech named his son Noah, and lived seven hundred seventy-seven years; 7 for those who would join to the Spirit of Christ must deliver peace to him, hoping in a God who helps those who take up and use his gifts.

8 By the Spirit of Christ Noah planted a vineyard, and having been found naked, cursed his son in Canaan. 9 For those who give not place to joy have no part in the wedding feast of the Lamb. 10 By the Spirit of Christ Terah accompanied Abram to Haran, for he saw that Abram had been called from his father's house; 11 and he would leave his land to be identified with one separated by God, if only to die on the way. 12 By the Spirit of Christ Abram separated from his nephew Lot, for though they were brethren, God said nothing in his appearing as to the seed of Lot. 13 By the Spirit of Christ Isaac blessed Jacob, sending him into the land of Padan-Aram to find a wife, for he accepted the judgment of God and his wife regarding Esau. 14 For he that would be found among Christ's mighty men must hate his own father, and mother, and wife, and children, and brothers, and sisters, and even his own life too; 15 abiding faithful to the journey given him by God.

16 By the Spirit of Christ Jacob took hold on his brother's heel. 17 By the Spirit of Christ he stole the birthright, advantaging himself of the towel wrapped about his brother's gifts, 18 for it is written, "Unto him that has, shall be given, and from him that has

not, shall be taken even what he seems to have." 19 By the Spirit of Christ Jacob set up, as a pillar, the stone he had made a pillow, vowing to give God a tenth of all, by which he lost Rachel. 20 By the Spirit of Christ he removed Laban's flock to himself, knowing that riches are for those who are rich toward God. 21 By the Spirit of Christ he took his family back to the land of promise, not hesitating at the threat of his brother, for God had said that he would be with him; 22 so he turned back the heart of his brother and the four hundred men with him through the gift he sent ahead. 23 By the Spirit of Christ he wrestled with the Angel and prevailed. 24 By the Spirit of Christ he limped to Shechem and destroyed the inhabitants of that wicked city. 25 For though the iniquity of the Amorite was not yet full, yet the zeal of Beth-el devoured his better judgment, and in his sons he delivered what God had begun at Sodom.

26 By the Spirit of Christ Joseph showed his brethren their father's heart, in which picture we see the patience of the Christ. 27 By the Spirit of Christ Moses slew the Egyptian, yet his own received him not until he came again with signs of power. 28 By the Spirit of Christ he smote the rock, calling them rebels who contended with him. 29 By the Spirit of Christ Caleb took Hebron, which later fell by lot to the Levites, leaving only for his inheritance its dependent villages.

30 By the Spirit of Christ Deborah prophesied that Jehovah would deliver Sisera into the hand of a woman, for she knew that glory is given by God to those who hesitate not to do his work. 31 By the Spirit of Christ Gideon taught the men of Succoth with the thorns of the wilderness. 32 By the Spirit of Christ Jepthah offered up his only daughter for a burnt offering. 33 By the Spirit of Christ he slew forty-two thousand men who could not rightly pronounce 'shibboleth,' for he who paid in full his vow to Jehovah might well remove those found at the marriage feast without a wedding garment. 34 By the Spirit of Christ Sampson

loved Delilah unto the telling of his Naziriteship, knowing that she would betray him, 35 for his soul was vexed unto death, and he would rather preserve his soul than gain the world. 36 By the Spirit of Christ he leaned on the pillars of the house of the Philistines, the lad guiding him, and slew more in his death than his life.

37 By the Spirit of Christ Boaz told Ruth not to glean in another's field, for those who have a care for the people of the Christ accept his companions as their own.

38 By the Spirit of Christ David faced the lion and the bear alone, for seeing a ruler insufficient for Jehovah's people, he was mindful to prepare himself to fill up what lacked. 39 By the Spirit of Christ he learned the harp while shepherding, by which skill he was brought even to the king's court. 40 For those that are Christ's love beauty; and he who received the pattern of the temple by the Spirit learned in youth the art of psalm, and of music, and of an excellent spirit; and he was loved by all the people. 41 By the Spirit of Christ he fled from Saul, gathering every man in Israel who was bitter of soul into a great camp, like the camp of God; 42 and they became, in following him, the mighty men of Israel. 43 By the Spirit of Christ he asked to build a house for God, by which God made a covenant with him to build him an eternal house, from which is the Christ.

44 For the Spirit of Christ is the fellowship of all those who, finding themselves alone, embrace the circumstances of their earthly journey; who together make perfect the accomplishments of Jesus Christ, who perfects all things. 45 But if one does not persevere, he is like a thorn in the hand of a drunkard, that is not removed until the morning, and whose stock is fit only for the burning. 46 For no man, having put his hand on the plow, and looking back, is fit for the kingdom of the world of our Lord and his Christ.

8 We have then a Stone, cut without hand, which smites all the kingdoms of the world and grinds them to powder; 2 which has filled the whole earth, and become a great mountain. 3 For in spirit we stand upon this mountain and view the bride, the Lamb's wife, 4 and here we see what we who have been made companions of the Christ have become. 5 Let each in particular beware unto himself that he fail not from this calling, for outside are the dogs, and the sorcerers, and the fornicators, and the murderers, and every one that loves, and makes a lie. 6 For Joab, who accompanied David in all his exploits, never lost in war; yet was killed holding on to the horns of the altar, 7 for he knew the heart of David, and respected it not. 8 Nor let any be desirous of godliness as if by it he increases; for also Balaam fell by this deceit, making an idol from the same stock of wood that he burned in the fire to warm himself. 9 For those who increase themselves cannot redeem themselves, having sold themselves to hypocrisy. 10 Nor will these in any way see the King in the day of the gladness of his heart.

11 The Lamb's wife comes up from the place prepared for her in the wilderness like pillars of smoke; and is seen coming down out of heaven from God, 12 having the glory of God, and the honor of the Lamb. 13 She rules the house of God, for by night her lamp goes not out. 14 Destruction and death have heard the report of her with their ears, yet no proud one has walked the path to her home. 15 If one need counsel, she speaks from herself. 16 If one lack maturity, the law of kindness is on her tongue. 17 She loves those that love her, and teaches the fear of Christ. 18 She laughs at the coming day, for her eyelids look forth as the dawn; 19 she is fair as the moon, clear as the sun, and terrible as troops with banners. 20 Many bright ones stand before the throne of the Lord of the whole earth, but she excels them all.

9 Remember Jesus in his last night, washing the feet of the disciples, and what he said to them late into the night. 2 For his ways are our ways, yet God's ways are not. 3 For he is like us, being found in fashion as a man; and we are like him, having been taken out of his side: 4 we are bone of his bone, and flesh of his flesh. 5 And having borne the condemnation for humility from God, and having had his ways seen of God and been healed, he brings us unto himself. 6 And coming to his dwelling, we find many abodes, and God himself, who will be to each one, God. 7 For he says, "Behold, I make all things new." 8 And he wipes away all the tears of suffering, and all the weariness of spirit, brought about by those who love the Spirit of Jesus. 9 And to those that believe will be the blessing, who say to the Christ,

10 Yours we are Jesus,
And with you, O sent of the Father;
Peace, peace be to you
And peace to your helpers,
For your God helps you.

11 There the hungry will be filled, and the pure of heart see God. 12 There for all reproach will be found an exceeding great reward, and there is the spoil divided. 13 For he that came from above is above all, and that which he has heard and seen with his eyes he has spoken to us, that our fellowship would be with the Father, and with his son Jesus Christ. 14 For though it cost him the desire of his heart, he brings the humble to dwell before God, and with the poor in spirit he builds a house for God, 15 whose house are we: now, the assembly; then, the bride; ever, the fullness of him who fills all in all.

16 For God will bring us to Christ, and Christ will present us to himself; and seeing the fruit of the travail of his soul, will be satisfied. 17 And the testimony is sure, and the price of the covenant has been secured, having the seal of God. 18 And we have known his seal, for he has given to us of his Spirit. 19 And knowing that the Son of God has come, we have an understanding, and we know him that is true. 20 And we are in him that is true, in his son Jesus Christ. 21 For *this* is eternal life:

that we should know him, the only true God, and his son Jesus Christ.

22 The Father loves the Son, and has given all things into his hand. 23 And we have known Jesus Christ; the same yesterday, today, and forever; 24 and we have seen that all things abide in this sameness, especially his very own: his bone and his flesh.

10 For this reason have I written to you who possess the key of the word of prophecy; 2 that you do not hinder those who enter into the Spirit of Christ, and that you might repent and enter in yourselves. 3 For every one who takes away from the word of our hope, God will take away his part from the tree of life, and from the holy city, which are written in his book. 4 For the subject can no longer be hid: the Voice has said "Cry!" And I said, "What shall I cry?" 5 …That the word of God abides forever. 6 Brethren, consider this word, for the things of which we speak are now about to be manifest.

7 And he said, "Write; for these things are true and faithful." 8 And he says to me, 'It is done.' 9 He who receives the testimony of Jesus has set to his seal that God is true, who has given to us the word of this cry by his Spirit. 10 Nor gives he the Spirit by measure, for the Spirit searches all things, even the depths of God where is hid the mystery of the bride. 11 And he that has the bride is the Bridegroom: he is the Root and Offspring of David, the bright and morning star; 12 who, receiving the plans of the Temple of God, commits them to those who would remain after his being delivered up; 13 and has returned to the Father where he has prepared for us a place. 14 And as to the Father, both his and ours, *he* prepares the wedding feast of the Lamb. 15 Eat, O friends; drink, yes, drink abundantly, beloved ones.

The Story in the Book of Hebrews

Abstract

God created this universe. God knows all things. God is unchangeable. But we find him getting involved in it at the strangest times and in the strangest ways. He gets upset. He gets pleased. He repents that he has made man. He does a host of things that an Eternal God, in our minds, has no business doing. Sometimes he interferes, sometimes he is aloof. This makes no sense to us, be we atheist, priest, truck driver, or all three.

There are, however, places in the bible, such as Isaiah 40-42, Job 37-38, and Deuteronomy 32, which take up this very subject and present us with a story that shows both sides of God in perfect harmony.

And then there is Hebrews.

Hebrews presents this dichotomy, not in God, but in his *Son*. Simultaneously, Hebrews presents *us* in that very same duality. Then it links us to his Son, which links us to God, putting the whole problem neatly on our laps with the question, "Now. What are you going to do about it?"

When we are faced with the Son, who both made the world and suffered in it, who both holds together all things by the word of his power, and was held to a cross with nails, we begin to see the enormity of our calling... and our opportunity. This is needed.

This is an exegesis of Hebrews... and its answer to this impossible duality.

Introduction

We will be going through the book of Hebrews in a straightforward manner and looking at what the author is saying, and why he chose all his particular words, quotes, and subjects. This book is so rich and concentrated that a single exegesis if it is to be readable must focus on one aspect; in this case his message. Two themes, which can be seen as the <u>rest of apostleship</u> and the <u>service of priesthood</u>, define the book. We will find that without addressing *both* of these personally we have no place with God. At times these two themes are described one at a time (often at length), sometimes paired in successive and dizzying rapidity, but ultimately tied together into a single unit which shows our full standing before God, and for that matter, his Son's.

Anyone could agree that the beginning litany attributed to the Son, followed by two chapters of scattered fragments from the Old Testament, are not random. But *how* are they not random, and *what* exactly is the writer trying to say? By looking at *what it actually says*, we can precisely draw out what he is saying... and in the process see why he is putting it in that most peculiar manner. Apostleship and Priesthood are diametrically opposed; the first is our powerful faith in joining in with the work of God in building his house, the second is our appointment to suffer along with his people within that house.

The fact that it is addressed *To The Hebrews*, in itself is most telling... he does not address them like James, "to the twelve tribes" or call them "Israel" as Paul often does, or even "Jews", which is common throughout, especially in the Gospels. The term "Hebrews" is found thrice: once in Acts where there is a dispute, and once each in 2 Corinthians & Philippians, in the same context of Paul defending his religious pedigree. And the singular, "Hebrew" is only used to describe the language, never a person.

Oh. And the author is deliberately anonymous, even though he's obviously writing to people who know who he is, as we can tell from the 'farewell' section. That was not something one did with a formal treatise of this nature. John did it, but John is weird. Add to this the fact that this book was one of the last books of the New Testament, meaning that the author was familiar with the bulk of what we call the New Testament. Just like us, only to him they were fresh.

So we are faced with an enormous amount of information <u>before we even begin reading the text</u>. And unless we think that the book refers to an obscure bunch of Jews in early Christianity, note that the writer purposely uses a term that refers to a kind of people that existed *before Abraham*. It refers to, as the Koran would put it, "People of the Book." Noah's death coincides with Abraham's birth, and Abraham in his life could have talked to all of Noah's descendants except his grandfather Nahor and Peleg. Those of this genealogy were likely the keepers of the documents (including the book of Enoch) that Noah brought with him from the old world. Yet while Abraham's family were 'People of the Book', he need to be called *out* of that community to start a new one. They had ceased to be effective apostles or priests, as evidenced from the character of Bethuel's family, especially Laban. They had lost the two kinds of faith required to follow God: the faith of companionship, and the faith of obedience.

Today, it would specifically be addressed to *those who have a heritage of Christianity, and are confident in that heritage*. And we who fall into that category are in the same danger of allowing our heritage to blind us from both the courage to be a "companion of the Christ" in building his house with him, and the humility to be "priests of God" in operating in his house with him. Hebrews is for <u>us</u>.

So without further ado, let us dive right in like the text itself does.

Part 1: It takes him two and a half chapters to get to his introductory point. And with good reason.

"**God.**" In serious literature, one does *not* begin with the Big Bang for the first word unless we are claiming a *comprehensive take on the subject*. Other than seven Psalms, no other book of the Bible attempts this. First Chronicles does it with Adam, almost. Many Psalms *address* Jehovah straight off, but not as subject matter; **Psalm 50** nails it, as does **Psalm 90**. Together they practically lay out the two themes of Hebrews. Then we have **93, 94, 97** (quoted by Hebrews), **99**, and **110** (quoted extensively by Hebrews) complementing them. And there are numerous quotes from this block of Psalms, 90-112, throughout Hebrews.

(1:1) God, having spoken of old to the fathers, in the prophets, by many portions and in many ways, has at the end of these days spoken to us in Son,

Note that God has spoken to us "in Son". The word "the" is not in there. It is like if i said i was going to paint this painting "in Blue". It is both him *and* his character by which God has spoken via the incarnation. And those to whom God was speaking are not the world or mankind or anything of the like; it is the fathers. These are the same fathers whose faith Paul says we are grafted into in Romans 11. And this tradition of faith of the fathers does not just go back, as Matthew says, to Abraham, it also does not just go back to Adam. The end of Luke 3 points out that it goes back to *God*. There is something about the faith of the fathers throughout history that shares the very faith that God had, that it would ultimately be worth it to make his creation in this manner (allowing sin). The changes from knowledge of this fact are so extensive that it was unspoken until the Son presented it. Jesus showed us how to share God's faith in him. Who is this 'us'? The audience of Hebrews is *those who keep the tradition of faith*. This is not a gospel tract.

(3) whom he appointed heir of all, through whom also he made the ages; who being the Glory's effulgence, and very image of his substance, and upholding the 'all things' by the word of his power, when he had made purification of the sins, sat down on the right of the Majesty on high;

Seven punches in a row to complacency. The "heir" takes us to Jesus' parable, "this is the heir, come let us kill him and the inheritance will be ours." Right away the reader is put on notice that he may be *in the very same position as the leaders of Israel to whom Jesus spoke these words*, i.e, "The law and the prophets were until John: from that time the glad tidings of the kingdom of God are announced, and every one forces his way into it." Forcing our way into the kingdom of God means obtaining it without faith. And assenting to the truth of the scriptures is <u>not</u> faith; the Pharisees did that. Believing in God is <u>not</u> faith, the demons do that. Faith, then, is the *fellowship with God in his works (the substantiating of things hoped for)* combined with the *living patiently within those works (conviction of things not seen)*.

"...Through whom also he made the ages" as in "Father of Eternity (the Age)" in Isaiah 6. This is specifically paired with "heir" to present the question, "What good is it to inherit it if you have made it in the first place?" This kind of question wants brought up before it can be answered, which is why the writer is pairing off dissonant ideas. In the next trilogy of superlatives he does the same thing: "who being (1) the Glory's effulgence, (2) and very image of his substance, (3) and upholding the 'all things' by the word of his power, —note the discordant idea next — when he had made purification of the sins, —and the return to the theme— (4) sat down on the right of the Majesty on high." We have four amazing descriptions of the Son, and *one* which brings the uncomfortable idea of his suffering to mind, *which does not seem to fit at all if the writer is sticking to the subject*. He is bringing in another subject and banging it into the first to wake us up to his theme.

Now since his thesis is God's ways of speaking, he gets right down to that. When God sends a message, he uses a messenger, which is literally what 'angel' means. Also notice he is simply expanding on the Gordian Knot he just gave us. Starting with "whom he appointed **heir** of all", he says of the *other* messengers:

(4) having become by so much better than the angels, as he hath **inherited** a more superior name than they. For to which of the angels did he ever say,
      You are my Son, I today have begotten you?

(Note that Psalm 2 describes the Sonship of *incarnation*, not eternal Sonship, as laid out in verse 3. The writer is presenting two—in our minds—conflicting ideas by presenting his eternal character, as in verse 3, and backing it up with verses presenting his incarnation.)

(5) and again,
      I will be to him Father, and he shall be to me Son?

(The phrase just before this passage in both 2 Samuel and 1 Chronicles is, "*He it is that shall build a house for me*" which will turn out to be the theme of this whole introduction.)

(6) And again, when he brings in the firstborn into the inhabited (earth) he says,
>And let all angels of God worship him.

(Here we have the reversal. Psalm 97 is clearly talking about Jehovah himself, yet it is applied to the firstborn brought into the world. Next in verse 8, he quotes the *future* blessing of God to the Son, in verse 10, the *past*, yet both give the dichotomy *as it already exists intact* in the quoted passage.)

(7) And of the angels he says,
>Who makes his angels spirits, and his ministers a flame of fire:

(In contrast with "*but a body have you prepared me*".)

(8) but of the Son,
>Your throne, O God, is unto the age of the age;
>And the scepter of uprightness is scepter of your kingdom.
>You have loved righteousness, and hated lawlessness;
>Therefore God, your God, has anointed you with oil of gladness above your companions.

(Note the very subtle introduction of a major subject. The contrast is between the angels and the Son, so who are these "*companions*"?)

(10) And,
>You, Lord, in the beginnings, did found the earth,
>And the heavens are works of your hands.
>They will perish, but you continue,

>And will all wax old as a garment;
>And as a mantle will you roll them up, as if a garment,
>And they will be changed; but you are the Same,
>And your years will not fail.

But of which of the angels has he ever said,
>Sit on my right hand till I make your enemies footstool of your feet?

Are they not all ministering spirits, sent forth unto service for them that will inherit salvation?

Okay. Big pause for breath here. Why keep talking about angels? All those scriptures about the Son *stand on their own* just fine. There was no need to contrast the Son with angels at every turn. And he is not even done with them yet. So what is going on? He does use them to make his first of many appeals to the reader in the next section, verses 2-4. But that alone is not sufficient reason to introduce the book with a treatise on angels.

In verse 5 of chapter 2 below, (foreshadowed by the hint of companions in verse 9 above,) he brings in the missing element: man. The situation he needs to emphasize is this: the angels are above us, and if we did not listen to their message, we died. He is above the angels, and if we do not listen to his message, we *really* die (as in, like, hell). But not only did he come to *deliver* a message; he *is* the message. "They said therefore to him, Who are you? Jesus said to them, Altogether that which I also say to you." But if he is the message, specifically when he became a man like us, lower than the angels whose message if we do not listen to we die, ...then we have got one really really confusing message here.

Well yes we do.

Do we see how the writer is building up *very deliberate contrasts* to make a *very difficult point*? After he has mentioned the angels eleven times in the first two chapters, they are *done*—all done—except for two references at the end of the book when he is tying things up. So as he leads up to the subject of Jesus, he makes absolutely sure that we understand the setting in which we humans (including Jesus) found ourselves, and that is <u>lower than the angels</u>. The ramifications are many, not the least of which is that we living are <u>still</u> lower than the angels, even if we expect one day to be higher. *Not in these bodies folks*. Which means that the message contained in the Law (spoken through angels) is not to be despised or discarded, but understood in the way that the new message (Christ) explains ...*But it is easier that the heaven and the earth should pass away than that one tittle of the law should fail.*

Now this law is the *outward* subject of much of Hebrews; indeed, most consider the book to be all about law and its place. And it is about that. But that is not the subject. Because if we do not understand our place in relation to the law (we are lower), then when someone blithely says, "We are saved, we are free from the law!" we might also assume that we are *above* the law. No, it is still there, and it is still more powerful than us, just like the angels who delivered it. True, we are not *under* law, but neither are we *over* it. There are actual relationships with it that we discover, such as: in order that the righteous requirement of the law should be fulfilled in us, who do not walk according to flesh but according to spirit. Paul is quite thorough on that subject. Hebrews *uses* this subject to point us on to things far better than merely our relationship with the law; the writer assumes that we have already read Paul whether we understood him or not.

But here we humans need introduced in proper perspective. Let us read on.

(2:1) Therefore we ought to give the more earnest heed to the things heard, lest possibly we drift away. For if the word spoken through angels became firm, and every transgression and disobedience received a just recompense of reward, how shall *we* escape, if we neglect so great a salvation? Which having at first been spoken through the Lord, was confirmed unto us by them that heard; the God bearing witness with them, both by signs and wonders, and manifold powers, and distributions of Holy Spirit, according to his will.

For not to angels did he subject the inhabited earth to come, whereof we speak. But one has somewhere testified, saying,
> What is man, that you remember him?
> Or the son of man, that you visit him?
> You made him little lower than angels;
> You crowned him with glory and honor,
> And did set him over the works of your hands:
> You did subject all things under his feet.

For in that he subjected the 'all things' to him, he left nothing not subject to him. But now we see not yet all things subjected to him. But we behold him who has been made a little lower than angels, Jesus, because of the suffering of the death, crowned with glory and honor; that by God's grace he should taste of death for every thing.

The writer is moving very rapidly here in dovetailing the transition from angels to men. And he drops a bombshell right where we would not expect; as a result we miss its vital placement. The first mention of Jesus in the book signals that we are going to be getting *personal* soon. Now that we have seen him thoroughly compared to *angels*, we are going to see him in his placement with *men*. Both of these are necessary before the writer can finish his introduction, as the former introduces his *Apostleship*, and the latter his *Priesthood*. And right away we get a shocking development: instead of *contrasts* as up until now, the writer has switched to *comparisons*. Do not the angels have more in common with the Son than men? Not according to the way this is being written.

(10) For it became him, for whom are the 'all things', and through whom are the 'all things', in bringing many sons unto glory, to perfect the author of their salvation through sufferings. For both the sanctifier and sanctified are all of one; for which cause he is not ashamed to call them brethren, saying,
> I will declare your name to my brethren,
> In midst of the church will I sing your praise.

And again,
> I will be trusting in him.

And again,
> Lo, I and the little children whom the God hath given me.

Since then the little children are sharers in blood and flesh, himself also in like manner partook of the same; that through the death he might bring to naught him that had the power of the death, that is, the devil; and might deliver all these who from fear of death were all their lifetime subject to bondage. For verily not to angels does he give help, but he gives help to the seed of Abraham. For this reason it behooved him in all things to be made like his brethren, that he might become a merciful and faithful high priest in the things pertaining to the God, to make propitiation for the sins of the people. For wherein himself has suffered being tempted, he is able to help those being tempted.

Big breath again. There was so much loaded into those verses, that one could write books on the doctrines. But the other New Testament writers already had, and the interest of Hebrews' writer is to *arrange* what we already have read as <u>doctrine</u>, into a <u>story</u>. So do not worry, we are not going to analyze "propitiation" or "the power of death"; John and Paul have covered that. But let us see what he just did.

Let us start with that phrase "are all of one". Sanctifier / sanctified... for whom / through whom... unto glory / through sufferings... are all of "One". One who, one what? We do not get that until verse four of the next chapter: "Who built all things is God." He is getting ready to finish his introduction, by presenting just exactly *what* is being built, and this will be the starting point for the book of Hebrews. It is *because of this thing being built* (for which cause) that Jesus is not ashamed to call us brethren.

But look what scriptures he quotes to back this up. The first one is from Psalm 22, *the most dramatic description of Jesus' sufferings in Psalms*. The next two are from Isaiah in the section in which it talks of him being a stumbling stone and a rock of offense, which Jesus quoted to his challengers. This is fellowship? This is brotherhood between us and Jesus? Now this is an important point, to which the writer will return later. <u>He is not ashamed to call us brethren because the thing that God is building puts us into the same place as him, and him into the same place as us</u>. The last section there elaborates, but remember, we are only in the introduction. *All* of this will be discussed in the text proper of Hebrews.

Note also that he finishes with the subject of angels with "For verily not to angels does he give help, but he gives help to the seed of Abraham." Does this make the angels inferior? No, it means that as regards what God is building, they do not require "help" to fulfill their part. On the other hand, the benefits that accrue from us *needing* this help are rather well beyond our imaginations.

Now he finishes his introduction, having taken us on a journey that whipped through psalm, doctrine, and history alike. He trusts that we are now aligned to <u>*be able to listen*</u> to the rest of the book. He trusts that the *terminology* has been aligned. And he trusts that the <u>issues</u> that are vital to understanding our place in the Great Story have been placed firmly into our minds.

(3:1) Whence, holy brethren, partakers of a heavenly calling, consider the **Apostle and High Priest** of our confession, Jesus; who was faithful to him that appointed him, as also was Moses in all his house. For he hath been counted worthy of more glory than Moses, by so much as he that built the house hath more honor than the house. For every house is built by some one; but who built all things is God. And Moses indeed was faithful in all his house as a servant, for a testimony of those things which were to be spoken; but Christ as a son, over his house; whose house are we, if we hold fast the boldness and the glorying of the hope firm unto the end.

As Apostle, he is sent by God to do his work. As High Priest he sees to it that we are included. This dual "appointment" will be thoroughly expanded on for the rest of Hebrews. Here, he mentions that Moses *also* had this same <u>dual</u> appointment. Now maybe we can start to see why Moses gave the Law. He was sent by God to do his work, which was getting Israel from Egypt to Canaan. As mediator between God and Israel (high priest in function), he had to see to it that God stayed with the people, and the people stayed with God. That God would go in their midst.

That Israel would approach God, as at Mount Sinai.

In other words, Moses had to *personally guarantee* the interests of both God and the people, and both of message and task. Jesus had to *personally guarantee* that God's work got accomplished, and that we would be included. We will find later in chapter 9, that this, <u>by definition</u>, produces the death of the guarantor (testator). Apostle and High Priest are 100% incompatible without the death of the person appointed to both roles. And before we get too weepy and praise-y about how wonderful it was for Jesus to do this, remember: this is *our* calling too. Moses gave the law because until some Apostle came along to make this calling remotely possible, *someone* needed to hold the position of high priest stable for the people. This someone was Law. Given from God by angels.

Now. We are told that Jesus was counted worthy of *more* glory than Moses, not because, as we suppose, he was just 'better', but because <u>the house Moses built did not include us</u>, Moses' house was part of the *larger* house that Jesus built. "And these all, having obtained witness through faith, did not receive the promise, God having foreseen some better thing for us, *that they <u>without us</u> should not be made perfect*." So if Moses was already part of a greater work that would make his own redundant, why would God appoint him to this role? Moses was, from the start, doomed to **(1)** his own death as its guarantor, or testator, **(2)** the eventual destruction of his work in bringing Israel to the Promised Land, and **(3)** the eventual putting away of the law he delivered, to be replaced with something better.

Well, remember what God said about Pharaoh? "And for this very cause have I raised you up, to shew you my power; and that my name may be declared in all the earth." Now hop over a few pages and see what he said to Moses. "And he said, Behold, I make a covenant: before all your people I will do marvels that have not been done in all the earth, nor in any nation; and all the people in the midst of which you are shall see the work of Jehovah: <u>for a terrible thing it shall be that I will do with **you**</u>." Now that had to hurt. *He was doing the same thing with Moses as he was doing with Pharaoh.* <u>Now</u> where are all the people who complain about not being able to resist his purposes? God may "set 'em up and knock 'em down" —those are the cards we are dealt. We can not ask for a re-deal. *It is what we <u>do</u> with those cards that define what people so ignorantly call 'freewill'.* There is yet more to this picture, as the relentless author of Hebrews will continue to tell us further on.

But before we leave this setup into which God placed Moses, look at the most peculiar place to put "but who built all things is God." Here is the unequivocal statement that God deals the cards, *including those which were dealt to the Son*. Notice that we are made "partakers of a heavenly <u>calling</u>" before we are "<u>appointed</u>". Moses asked for the job by siding with Israel and killing the Egyptian when he went out to look on his people. The son says, "Here am I. Send me." Just like Jonah, we may not like the job once we take it, but we had better live up to our agreement with God and do it.

So it is not a 'set-up'. Pharaoh picked his fate by becoming Pharaoh. Perhaps it would be better called an 'agreement'. Actually at the very end of this book, the author mentions, quite specifically, (supposing that by then we will have gotten the idea) that it is called the "Eternal Covenant".

And he ends his introduction by first gently reminding us how Moses took up the job. "Moses was <u>indeed</u> faithful in all his house" ...not for a testimony of those things that were to *happen*, but of "those things which were to be *spoken*". As in this very book.

So he saves the great surprise for the last line of his introduction. "Whose house are we." But only if we if we hold the boldness (Apostleship) and glorying (Priesthood) of the hope (God's house) firm unto the end. We are brought to the subject of the House of God. And it turns out that it is made of people. He started that paragraph by saying, "consider". He is not teaching doctrine here, he is telling a story. For the rest of Hebrews, the writer is going to "consider" quite a few very strange things. Doctrinally, he is rambling. But in storytelling, which is the way scripture teaches, he is opening up the reality behind all of creation, including what every day of our lives has to do with it.

The 'Great Story' behind Hebrews is now introduced. The positions are set up, the players are set up, and the stage is set. The next two chapters will show us the full story of **Apostleship**, which stretches from creation to judgment. Then the writer turns to **Priesthood**, which threatens the very fabric of who we believe God to be. But let us just dive in again…

End of Part 1
Take-aways:
- God is using a new language, speaking to us *in Son*.
- The Son has more in common with us than the angels who are higher than us.
- God is building something in which Jesus involves us.
- The two roles in which we join Christ are Apostle and High Priest.
- In the rest of this story we are going to be 'considering' these two roles.

Part II The Pool of Siloam: Apostleship

The beginning of the *text proper* of Hebrews is crisp and direct. If the reader has not paid attention up till now, the next two chapters will simply read, "Don't have a hard heart, or you won't enter into God's rest, which is probably heaven." Nothing could be farther from the truth. We note here that the writer of Hebrews (and even more so John), deliberately presents his ideas in such a way that *if the reader is unwilling to believe the words, or wants to read them objectively for his own gain, he will not understand them*. This is one of the great strengths of scripture. The Masons won't give you their secrets until you advance through enough degrees, earning the right to hear them. But God lays all his secrets out in the open in his word, just as he has done with nature, showing us that faith is not only necessary to approach him, it is necessary to understand anything at all.

Since 'being sent' is key to Apostleship, and as we have seen in the last section that even the distinction between when God 'calls' and when he 'appoints' us is vital, let us look at Paul's ordering of these. "How then shall they **call** upon him in whom they have not believed? and how shall they **believe** on him of whom they have not heard? and how shall they **hear** without one who preaches? and how shall they **preach** unless they have been **sent**?" That passage applies to us. As to God's calling *us*, notice how often,, when Paul introduces himself, he does not just say "apostle", he says "called apostle" as here from Romans: "Paul, bondman of Jesus Christ, called apostle, separated to God's glad tidings".

And because "Many are called, but few are chosen", God "has called us with a *holy* calling", or a "heavenly calling" as we just had at the end of the introduction. Peter adds to this that God has "called us by glory and *virtue*", so John puts it together as follows, "and they with him are called, <u>and</u> chosen <u>and</u> faithful". All three. But let's look at that far rarer expression 'appointed' from "consider the Apostle and High Priest of our confession, Jesus; who was faithful to him that **appointed** him" from the Introduction.

Now. There is just one person in the New Testament who is spoken of as being **appointed** in the same way as Moses was appointed in the *Old*. To this person was given both a specific *unique message* and a specific *intercessory role* as concerns the Gospel. In other words, he was to be the **Apostle** and **Herald** of the gospel to the *nations*. Here it is:

...gospel; to which *I* have been <u>appointed</u> **herald** and **apostle** and **teacher** of nations. For which cause also I suffer these things…

...for God is One, and Mediator of God and men, one man; Christ Jesus, who gave himself a ransom for all, the testimony in its own times; to which *I* have been <u>appointed</u> **herald** and **apostle**. *I speak the truth, I do not lie*, a **teacher** of nations in faith and truth.

For I speak to you, the nations, inasmuch as *I* **am apostle of nations**, I glorify **my ministry**, if by any means I will **provoke to jealousy…**

What? Does this mean the Gospel to the Nations belongs to *him personally*? Paul?

…in day when God shall judge the secrets of men, according to **my gospel** by Jesus Christ.

Now to him that is able to establish you, according to **my gospel** and the preaching of Jesus Christ, according to revelation of mystery, kept silent through the times of the ages, but has now been made manifest, and by prophetic scriptures, according to the commandment of the Eternal God, is made known for obedience of faith **to all the nations** unto obedience of faith…

Remember Jesus Christ raised from among dead, of seed of David, according to **my gospel**, in which I suffer even unto bonds as an evil-doer: but the word of God is not bound.

…according to the gospel of the glory of the blessed God, **with which *I* have been entrusted**.

…if so you continue in the faith, founded and firm, and not moved away from the hope of the gospel, which you have heard, proclaimed in the whole creation under the heaven, **of which *I* Paul became minister**. Now, I rejoice in the sufferings for you, and fill up on my part that which is lacking of the afflictions of the Christ in my flesh, for his body, which is the church, of which *I* became minister, according to the dispensation of God, **given me towards you, to complete the word of God**.

…but in his own season manifested his word in proclamation, **with which *I* have been entrusted, according to the commandment of our Savior God**…

To **me**, less than the least of all saints, has this grace been given, to announce among the nations the gospel of the unsearchable riches of the Christ.

And yes, the "*I*" is emphatic in the Greek every time. We don't have a choice here. This language would be the height of arrogancy unless Paul was given a position of Apostle and Herald *that no one else* was given. A large and influential group of Jewish believers centered in Jerusalem took great exception to what they saw as Paul's arrogant excesses. 'Okay, so God wants to include some Gentiles; fine, but this is a *Jewish* religion. Moses set it up. Jesus fulfilled it. Now we're vindicated as the Chosen People, or alternatively, the Chosen among the Chosen, as not all of Israel believes yet.'

One can sympathize with them. God put up with that for about forty years, ironically the same as what we'll read when we get back to the text of Hebrews.

Space prohibits us here to look at Paul's testimony throughout Acts, and see the very real astonishment (by Festus) and anger (by Ananias) by which *every* effort was made to interrupt, silence, and kill Paul… not because he was an Apostle—there were plenty of them around and they were quite popular—but because of two things: (1) He was Apostle to the Nations, and (2) he had a specific personal **appointment** from Jesus himself, *that none of the others had*. These produced jealously in the extreme, *both to his person and his writings*. And please note that this jealousy was *not* coming from unbelievers.

This would mean that, like Moses, he would have a unique role in standing between Christ and the saints.

But for this reason mercy was shown me, **that in me, first, Jesus Christ might display the whole long-suffering**, for a delineation of those about to believe on him to life eternal. Now, I rejoice in the sufferings for you, and **fill up <u>on my part</u> that which is lacking of the afflictions of the Christ in my flesh, for his body**, which is the church.

For I am already **being offered**, and the season of my departure is come. The good fight I have fought, the course I have finished, the faith I have kept.

This would also mean that, like Moses, he would have been warned at the beginning as when Moses was warned, "for a terrible thing it shall be that I will do with you." And yes, Ananias was told "Go, for *he* is Chosen Vessel to me, to bear my name before both nations and kings and sons of Israel: for *I* will show to him how much he must suffer for my name."

This would also mean that *he personally* can take credit for presenting saints to Christ:

For I am jealous as to you with a jealousy of God; for I espoused you unto one husband, to present *pure virgin* to the Christ.

...because of the grace given to me by the God, for me to be minister of Christ Jesus to the nations, carrying on as a sacrificial service the gospel of God, that the offering up of the nations might be acceptable, being sanctified by Holy Spirit, <u>I therefore have the boast in Christ Jesus</u> in the things which pertain to God.

This would also mean that just as Moses undertook a work that would eventually be swallowed up in the much greater work of Jesus ("by so much as he that has built the house has more honor than the house"), so Paul's life work and unique Gospel would be swallowed up by the much greater work of Christ.

...for I have wished, I myself, to be a curse from the Christ for my brethren, my kinsmen, according to flesh...

For also that glorified is not glorified in this respect, on account of the surpassing glory.

For we know in part, and we prophesy in part; but when that which is perfect has come, that which is in part shall be done away.

For I would not, brethren, have you ignorant of this the Mystery, lest you be self deluding, that hardening in part has befallen the Israel, until the fullness of the nations be come in; and so all Israel shall be saved.

This would also mean that there is a strange and great Mystery surrounding Christ's appointment of Paul to this singular Apostleship.

...the **Mystery** (as I have written before briefly, by which, in reading it, you can perceive my understanding in the **Mystery of the Christ**) which in other generations has not been made known to the sons of men, as it has now been revealed to his holy apostles and prophets in spirit, that the nations should be joint heirs, and joint body, and joint partakers of the promise in Christ Jesus **by the gospel of which I am become minister** according to the gift of the grace of the God **given to me**, according to the working of his power.

...which is the church; **of which *I* became minister**, according to the dispensation of God <u>given me toward you to complete the word of God</u>, the **Mystery** hid from the ages from the generations, but has now been made manifest to his saints.

At this point, the Mystery of the entire chapter of Ephesians three is beginning to make an enormous amount of sense. We have an unnamed Mystery that spans the ages, we have someone picked out like Moses to present it, both in word of ministry and personal experience, we have a Gospel which belongs to him, in which is hidden this Mystery, and we have all this in context by Paul's own words.

We have the key to the Mystery.

Now let's go to the "text proper" of Hebrews. It begins in Chapter three, verse seven.

The writer begins right off with the last half of the 95th Psalm. It's worth reading for comparison.

Psalm 95

1 Come, let us sing aloud to Jehovah,
   Let us shout for joy to the rock of our salvation;
2 Let us come before his face with thanksgiving;
   Let us shout aloud unto him with psalms.
3 For Jehovah is a great God,
   And a great king above all gods.
4 In his hand are the deep places of the earth;
   The heights of the mountains are his also:
5 The sea is his, and he made it,
   And his hands formed the dry.
6 Come, let us worship and bow down;
   Let us kneel before Jehovah our Maker.
7 For he is our God;
   And we are the people of his pasture
       And the sheep of his hand.
   To-day if you hear his voice,

> 8   Harden not your heart as at Meribah,
>   As the day of Massah, in the wilderness;
> 9   When your fathers tempted me;
>   Proved me, and saw my work.
> 10 Forty years was I grieved with the generation,
>   And said, It is a people that do err in their heart,
>   And they have not known my ways;
> 11 So that I swore in mine anger,
>   That they should not enter into my rest.

(3:7) Because of this, even as the Holy, the Spirit, says,
Today if you will hear his voice,
Harden not your hearts, as in the provocation,
Like as the day of the trial in the wilderness,
Where your fathers tried, by proving,
And saw my works forty years,
Wherefore I was displeased with this generation,
And said, They always err at heart;
But *they* did not know my ways;
As I swore in my wrath,
If they shall enter into my rest,

Whoa. This *definitely* is not a gospel tract.

(12) See, brothers, lest possibly an evil heart of unbelief will be in any one of you, in the falling away from the Living God;

Okay. Let us see what we have here. 'Unbelief' is being equated with the *deliberate* hardening of their hearts, not simple ignorance, going beyond evil into what scripture calls wickedness. Peter had said, "Be saved *from* this perverse generation." Then what is "Today"? It is in contrast with "the day of the trial in the wilderness" in which they *could* not hear, because "*they* did not know my ways." Since "the faith therefore is by hearing, and the hearing by Christ's word," as Jesus says, "Why do you not know my speech? Because you cannot hear my word", so they, in "the day of the trial in the wilderness" were "shut out from belief" because they could not even hear, which is required if one is to know what to believe.

And it is more evident that there were those who *could* hear, and those that could not. As to Caleb and Joshua, who heard and believed that "the day of the trial in the wilderness" *was* "Today" for they *did* know his ways, as says Caleb, "If Jehovah delight in us, he will bring us into this land." But those who "were not united by faith with them that heard" defaulted to self-imposed obedience (or disobedience); since they had rejected fellowship belief was relegated to opinion, and obedience to how much respect each was deemed to have. Those who were not united by faith to Moses had no option but to accept 'man's person' in each other, and "measuring themselves by themselves, and comparing themselves with themselves" were not wise; as says Jesus, "How *can* you believe, who receive glory one of another, and seek not the glory which is from God alone?"

But "how shall they believe on him of whom they have not heard? And how shall they hear without one who preaches? and how shall they preach unless they have been sent?" It was Moses who was sent to evangelize the children of Israel, but they were not "united in faith" with him, for their hearts were hardened. How does it come about that our hearts are hardened away from companionship with the evangelizer whom God sends? We do not understand God's ways. What is it about God's ways that we do not understand? We do not understand his rest.

We supposed that we were getting a 'free lunch' in having God's

Apostle lead us into salvation. But this is the deceitfulness of sin. For instead of fellowship *with* his Apostle, we look for yummies *from* him, and as a result treat God whom he came to reveal like Santa Claus instead of a Father looking for fellowship. "Verily, verily, I say to you, You seek me not because you have seen signs, but because you have eaten of the loaves and been filled. Work not for the food which perishes, but the food which abides unto life eternal, which the Son of man will give to you; for him has the Father sealed, the God." And this lack of fellowship, replaced by whining and murmuring for yummies against Moses, resulted in: "Hear now, you rebels, shall we bring forth to you water out of the rock?" as with Paul: "if I come again I will not spare."

So it is evident that "Today" is the day of our having fellowship with the one whom God sent, his Apostle. Let us go on with the text.

(13) but exhort one another each day, so long as it is called Today: lest anyone of you be hardened by the deceitfulness of the sin:

And it is evident that we can help each other in this fellowship, as Caleb, the *only* one who initially spoke up, did with Joshua, who joined him subsequently.

(14) for we are become companions of the Christ, if indeed we hold fast the beginning of the confidence firm unto the end while it is said,
>Today if you will hear his voice,
>Harden not your hearts, as in the provocation.

Here the writer is quoting himself, only this time, instead of holding fast the "boldness and the glorying of the hope" as in the Introduction, it is simply "the confidence" to be held "firm unto the end." In the Introduction it was being his house, but here it is fellowship with his Apostle *from within that house*, but more; the willingness to join in the Sent One's efforts to build the house. *Now* we see the also-unique position of those like Caleb, John the Baptist, and Timothy. As regards Paul, they were *companions* of the apostle, as he says at one point, "Only Luke is with me."

And now we see our position with the "Apostle and High Priest of our confession, Jesus": companions. The 45th Psalm, from which this and the quote in the introduction (1:9) are taken, is a dramatic portrayal of the attitude taken by the companions of the Christ. If one is to engage in a true *apostolic work* (which the writer will sketch out in scary detail later in Hebrews), one must be a companion of the Apostle. And if history is anything by which to judge, *there has never been, at any point in history, sufficient companions to God, his Apostle of our faith Jesus, or any of the 'sent ones'*. In other words, if we are looking for fame and fortune in heaven, there's no line at the door. "Knock, and it will be opened to you."

If i may expand on that point for a moment before we go on. When John baptized Jesus, there was a dramatic opening of the heavens, Holy Spirit coming down on Jesus in visible form, and the very voice of God thundering down, "This is my beloved Son in whom I am well pleased." Now John had disciples. Lots of them. And he had been telling them and everyone else who came that there was Someone coming. Now go and read John chapter one. It was not until the *next day*, after the nudging of John the Baptist when he saw Jesus again, that two of John's disciples went up and asked him where he lived, and went and stayed with him that night. Two. The next day. No, there's not exactly a line at the door, unless there's free bread and fishes involved. Or healing. Or self-help armchair psychology.

(16) For who, when they heard, did provoke? No, not *all* that came out of Egypt by Moses. And with whom was he displeased forty years? Was it not with them that sinned, whose bodies fell in the wilderness? And to whom swore he that they should not enter into his rest, but to the disobedient? And we see that they could not enter because of disbelief.

The writer makes the point here that the only ones to whom the negative sense of "If they shall enter into my rest" applies, are the disobedient with whom God was displeased. He points this out because otherwise we might think that the "Today" or the "rest" is necessarily future. Note the irony in this as he is well aware that those who deprecate his writings are going to make God's rest a future event to excuse their own avoidance of it.

(4:1) Let us fear therefore, lets perhaps, a promise being left of entering into his rest, anyone of you should seem to have come short. For indeed we have been evangelized even as also they; but the word of the hearing did not profit them, because they were not united by the faith with them that heard.

Now the writer turns to the delicate task of pointing out that some in his audience were *obviously* drawing back, and others were obviously "united by the faith with them that heard". In the context of when this was written, the holders-back would be those who resisted Paul's gospel, as Peter says, "...according as our beloved brother Paul also has written to you according to the wisdom given to him, as also in all letters, speaking in them of these things; among which some things are hard to be understood, which the untaught and ill-established wrest, as also the other scriptures, to their own destruction." These were not "united by faith" with Paul, whose ministry clearly lays out the establishment of a new covenant apart from the one with Moses, by which one, by apprehending what God's true rest is, can rest from his own works, as later explained at the beginning of chapter six.

(3) For we enter into the rest who have believed, even as he has said,
>As I swore in my wrath,
>If they shall enter into my rest,

Although the works were finished from the world's foundation. For he has said somewhere of the seventh day thus:
>And the God rested on the seventh day from all his works.

Emphasis on the "rest" in the quote above, emphasis on the "if" in the quote below. First he points out that we're *not* talking about creation's rest, then points out that the use of the word "if" leaves room for some to *have* entered, and *to* enter that rest. He goes on to elaborate, jumping back on that word "Today":

(5) And in this, again:
>If they shall enter into my rest.

Since therefore it remains that some enter into it, and the previously evangelized entered not because of disobedience, he again defines a certain day, Today, saying in David so long a time after (even as has been said before),
>Today if you will hear his voice,
>Harden not your hearts.

Remarkable how the writer keeps pounding this point home, indicating equally how much we need it, and how fiercely it will be attacked. What is the Today based on? Not *when* we hear his voice, but "**if you will** hear his voice". We will *not*, is the insinuation. And even if we *will*, we will harden our heart immediately after hearing it. And by the way, when he speaks of being angry with "your fathers" "in the wilderness", then says "Wherefore I was displeased with this generation", it is not *that* generation, it is *this* generation. While he is talking about being displeased with *them*, he is simultaneously talking about being displeased with *us* for seeing the lesson that they went through and ignoring it. The anger is *right here, right now*. "Today" is mentioned five times in this section and two more later in the epistle when he turns the application to Jesus himself.

And the writer does not miss a trick. "Saying in David" ...why mention him, other than the fact that he wrote the psalm? David has the longest list of named *companions* in the entire Bible. They are his mighty men, and without them, his six and a half year civil war that ripped the fledgling nation of Israel apart might have lasted considerably longer. And if he had had more of them it could have been considerably shorter. And this is what is needed today. Can we go down into a pit and kill a lion on a snowy day? How about kill 800 men in hand-to-hand combat at one time? But the question for us is not *can* we, but *are we willing?* Today if you *will* hear his voice…

(8) For if Joshua had given them rest, he would not have spoken afterward of another day,

...and he puts the last nail in the coffin by explaining that we can not call the "rest" the *promised land* either (for us this is somewhat akin to considering the rest to be heaven). What he has been so careful to do is to take a prophetic scripture and point out that there is absolutely no context in which this mystical "Today" can be taken other than *God's rest in the finished work of Christ*. The writer thoroughly fleshes this out much later in the end of chapter nine. Here he is just going to give us the bottom line:

(9) A sabbath rest remains therefore for the people of the God. For who is entered into his rest has himself also rested from his work, as the God did from his own. Let us therefore give diligence to enter into that rest, that no one fall after the same example of the disobedience.

Since the writer does not see fit (for another five chapters) to explain just exactly how one can rest from his work, we'll follow suit. But we can consider what rest actually is by understanding what *work* is and is not. God rested on the seventh day because creation was *finished*. Now he could *do something* with his earth. If we spent six years building a house, and were finished on the seventh, would we have no more use for the house? Rest means *using* the thing we have been *working* on. Rest is when the fun starts. It does not mean going to sleep, it means hopping into that Ferrari that we've been building for so long and *going somewhere*. Ripping up the streets in our Ferrari is not *work*. Building it was. Ripping up the streets is *rest*.

That is very simple. But think about the contemporary ideas about having a relationship with God. "Ah, now we are 'saved', we do not have to *do* anything!" Or, "My final resting place will be in heaven!" No, that is when we *start* doing things. <u>To be a companion of the Christ is to finally have finished with the process of approaching God (by having gotten there, by Jesus) so that we and Christ and God can finally *do* things together</u>, i.e., build his house. Those who deny this have a good reason to. <u>It hurts</u>. Much later, the writer will get to "you have not yet resisted unto blood, wrestling against sin." Sorry guys, but *it is going to hurt a lot worse if we do not resist to blood*. To actively engage with God is, yes, to hurt; the difference is that *we have control over the hurt*. The marathon runner hurts to get to the finish line first, but that is a much better hurt than having our telly roll off the shelf onto our head while we are sleeping. Let us say that the marathon runner and the sleeper received the same amount of pain. Whom would we rather be?

(12) For living is the Word of the God, and active, and sharper than any two-edged sword, and piercing even to the dividing of soul and spirit, of both joints and marrow, and a discerner of thoughts and intents of the heart. And there is no creature not manifest in his sight; but all things are naked and laid open before the eyes of him with whom we have to do.

His summary paragraph broadsides the reader with the word of God seemingly out of nowhere, and does not let up. Where did that come from? He has just clearly differentiated companionship from disobedience. And now we have a new player, a new Being Who Is Alive, that we were hoping was just a bunch of words we could study at our leisure. No, *his* name is The Word of God. Read what it *literally* says. He is alive. He is active. He discerns. His sight manifests everything. The writer's message is that those who think they can pick and choose over what parts of the Gospel (another sentient being by the way), or pick and choose what version of the Gospel to believe, are fooling *no one*.

The Pharisees once asked Jesus, "Are we blind too?" His reply was, "If you were blind, you would have no sin. But now you say, 'We see'; Your sin remains." The blind man had been sent to the Pool of Siloam. A pool is a place of rest. Siloam means 'rest'.

But notice he has not said *what* the Word of God will do to the willingly disobedient. The use of the phrase "whose bodies were strewn in the desert" is all he gives for now. But to continue our habit of watering down, or making into a metaphor, everything in scripture is not historically wise. Historically, shortly after Hebrews was written, Jerusalem was sacked. Do we think this cannot happen to Christianity? "So because you are lukewarm, and neither hot nor cold, I am about to spew you out of my mouth." Not "I might," but "I am about to".

End of Part II

Take-aways:
- Enter into God's rest now or perish.
- Apostleship (a *sent one*) is someone sent from God for a specific reason at a specific time with a specific message.
- Moses as an apostle gave the law and insured that God would go in Israel's midst. Jesus as an apostle brought to light life and incorruptibility. Paul as an apostle presented the gospel and the mystery.
- We can not hear what God actually says if we willfully disbelieve. Unbelief is willful.
- We do not enter into God's rest when we do not listen to what God actually says.
- The Word of God will getcha if'n you don't watch out.

Part III The Great High Priest
Section I Melchizedek and the Law
(Section II will be The Eternal Covenant)

The subject of high priest had been introduced in 2:17 at the end of the contrast with angels and comparison with humans with the remarkable statement "Thus it behooved him in all things to be made like his brethren, that he might become a merciful and faithful high priest in the things pertaining to God, to make propitiation for the sins of the people. For in what he has suffered being tempted, he is able to help those being tempted." Now we get that same high priest introduced as having "passed through the heavens".

(4:14) Having therefore a great high priest who has passed through the heavens, Jesus the Son of the God, let us hold fast the confession.

This is a strange way to introduce him. Why not 'spent time on earth' or 'gone into the heavens'? Why does he say "passed through the heavens"? The writer goes on to reiterate the substantial point of being tempted just as we are tempted, preventing us from attributing some 'magical aloofness' to Jesus.

(15) For we have not a high priest that cannot sympathize with our infirmities, but one in all tempted according to our likeness, without sin.

The writer says "passed through" because he is moving on from what he stated in 1:3, "when he had made purification of the sins, sat down on the right of the Majesty on high" and is presenting the Priest who is there "to make propitiation for the sins of the people" as 2:17 stated. He is not in a position to "make propitiation *for* the sins" (literally, *propitiating the sins*) until after he has "made purification *of* the sins". The passing through the heavens is *on his way to God* where he "sat down on the right of the Majesty on high". This purifying of the sins has to come first, and the writer of Hebrews clearly states at the beginning of chapter six that this is *not* his subject. In other words, if we are still worried about how Jesus "purified" our sins (not *us*, our *sins*; purification of *us* is yet another subject), we will not be able to even consider why or how it is necessary to "make propitiation for the sins".

This is no small point, and without it we do not have access to the confidence necessary to approach God's throne, as he says next.

(16) Let us therefore with boldness approach the throne of the grace, that we may receive mercy and find grace to help in time of need.

Purification of sins is different from them being "washed away" as Acts 22:16, or washing us "from our sins" as Revelation 1:5, or getting rid of the dirt on our feet as Jesus did with his disciples, but the *making of the sins themselves into something different than what they had been, by placing those actions which were sins into a completely different context in which those same actions are no longer sins because they have been purified*. What is this strange and new context? When we lived in sins (actions that could never be perfected and so must be condemned) we lived without faith (that we could do perfect things) or hope (that someone could use our mistakes for good).

We just got through a chapter and a half of talking about God's rest and the requirement that we *fellowship* with God and his sent one(s). This is why that chapter used the phrase, "united by faith". When *we* find that we cannot finish or perfect what we do, it is appropriate to look for someone who *can*. Or at the least, go to our Creator and ask him what to do. When we go to God and ask we discover that he has already been working on the problem for some time. But God is in heaven, and we are on earth; all his help is one-directional. We needed one who was *sent* (<u>away</u> from God, <u>to</u> us) to be able to make this work operate in both directions: (1) from God to us, and (2) from us to God.

Jesus said "My food is that I should do the will of him that has sent me, and that I should **finish** his work." What was the work of God? "Jesus answered and said to them, This is the work of God, that you believe on him whom *he* has sent." When we are "united by faith" with Jesus, all our actions become associated with his. Jesus tells the story of a man who built a tower and could not complete it. This is like our sins: all the imperfect and incomplete actions in our life. If we join a team of tower-builders with Jesus as the superintendent, he sees to it that every tower gets completed to full specifications and beyond. He also sees to it that everyone on his team is at full efficiency. "Every branch in me not bearing fruit, he takes it away; and every one bearing fruit, he purges it that it may bring forth more fruit. You are already clean by reason of the word which I have spoken to you. Abide in me and I in you. As the branch cannot bear fruit of itself unless it abide in the vine, thus neither you unless you abide in me. I am the vine, you the branches. He that abides in me and I in him, *he* bears much fruit; for without me you can do nothing. Unless any one abide in me he is cast out as the branch, and is dried up; and they gather them and cast them into the fire, and they are burned. If you abide in me, and my words abide in you, you will ask what you will and it will come to pass to you. In this is my Father glorified, that you bear much fruit, and you will become disciples of mine."

The word "finish" was bolded in the above paragraph because Jesus already did it. "It is finished." This is *purification* of sins. It is the finished work of Christ that God does not have to work on anymore. It is the rest of God. He does not have to decide whether a branch belongs in the vine or not: Christ has taken care of that. All God has to do is see if it is bearing fruit or not, and act accordingly. This removing of useless branches and pruning of useful ones is what propitiation *for sins* is about. It is directly responsible for God's patience with us, and not with only us, but the whole world. The writer assumes that we are already familiar with purification (but does mention that we have forgotten in the next chapter), and goes on to talk about *propitiating the sins*, which is the two-way back and forth between what we are clumsily doing badly and what Christ is showing God: that the things that we are doing will actually work out for good because of how he is handling it. Why is this position of a mediator (as Paul calls it) necessary? Because unlike Jesus, we have *not* yet "passed through the heavens".

The qualifications for such a position are intricate. Jesus was not interested in mediating between a perfect God and a system which perfected nothing (the law). "Man, who made me judge or divider over you?" The mediation is not between good and evil, the law and lawlessness, sin and righteousness, but *God and man*. This brings us back to the text, where the writer begins his outline of what this involves. And note that the writer consistently uses *all* of human history—not just the New Testament—when making his points. He freely uses physical interpretation, spiritual interpretation, comparison, contrast, and types (from which we get the word 'archetype') in dizzying succession. A much longer paper than this one could be written just on his writing protocols. But here we are focused on the point of what he is saying.

(5:1) For every high priest, being taken from men, is appointed for men in things relating to God, that he may offer both gifts and sacrifices for sins; who can bear gently with ignorant and erring since he himself also is compassed with infirmity; and by it is bound, as for the people, so also for himself, to offer for sins. And no one takes the honour to himself but when called of God, even as also was Aaron. So Christ also glorified not himself to become high priest; but who spoke unto him,
>   *You* are my Son,
>   *I* today have begotten you;
as he says elsewhere,
>   You are priest unto the age
>   After the order of Melchizedek.

This "*I* today have begotten you" is loaded. We asked the question in the last section, What is the Today based on? Not *when* we hear his voice, but "**if you will** hear his voice". Now God returns this to Jesus: I have heard *your* voice, which he goes on to expand.

(7) Who in the days of his flesh, having offered up prayers and supplications with strong crying and tears to him who was able to save him from death, and having been heard because of his godly fear; though he was Son, yet learned obedience by what he suffered; and. perfected, he became unto all that obey him, author of eternal salvation, named of God high priest after the order of Melchizedek.

This being perfected is what Jesus spoke of when he said "Behold, I cast out demons and accomplish healings today and tomorrow, and the third I am perfected; neverless, I must go on today and tomorrow and the following." Until the work of God, which involved the consciousness on the part of his companions of him being sent from God as well as the placing of them outside of the law's condemnation of sin, was finished, he would not enter the foretold death that put an end to "the days of his flesh" and begin his own work. In regards to his mortal life he had said "For also the things concerning me have an end." And he took his time before he ascended and "passed through the heavens", appearing to various individuals and groups at his leisure; and we are given no explanation of what was in his mind or what he was to be accomplishing at the time; only that we observe a peculiar freedom similar to when a particularly long and drawn out job is finally finished.

These are things that he wants to enjoy with us. But we do not participate. The writer is constrained to stop and point this out. His audience (the shoe fits; put it on) can not understand him because they are babes even though it is time to be adults. Further, they are bored with the subject and not bearing any fruit. Further, this path gets one burned up. Note that at the end, he says he is persuaded better things of them—not because they *can* understand him, not because they are *not* sluggish—but because at least physically they have shown a bit of fruit: ministering to the saints. The branch does not get cut off and thrown into the fire just yet.

(11) Concerning whom we have much to say, and hard of interpretation, since you are become dull in hearing. For when for the time you ought to be teachers, you have again need that someone teach you the rudiments of the beginning of the oracles of God, and are become such as have need of milk, not solid food. For every one that partakes of milk is inexperienced in

word of righteousness, for he is a babe. But the solid food belongs to full-grown men, who, by reason of use, have their senses exercised to discern both good and evil. For this reason leaving the word of the beginning of the Christ, let us be carried on unto the perfection; (not laying again a foundation of repentance from dead works, and of faith toward God—the teaching of baptisms, and of laying on of hands, and of resurrection of dead, and of eternal judgment) and this will we do, if only God permit. For as to those who were once enlightened and tasted of the heavenly gift, and became partakers of Holy Spirit, and tasted the good word of God, and the powers of the age to come, and fell away, it is impossible to renew again unto repentance; they crucifying again to themselves and openly shaming the Son of God. For land which drinks the rain that comes often upon it, and brings forth herbs fitting for them for whose sake it is also tilled, receives blessing from God: but if it bears thorns and thistles, it is disapproved and near a curse; whose end is to be burned. But of you, beloved, we are persuaded better things and having salvation, even if we thus speak: for God is not unrighteous to forget your work and the love which you showed toward his name, in that you ministered unto the saints, and do minister. And we desire that each of you show the same diligence unto the fullness of the hope even to the end: that you be not sluggish, but imitators of them who through faith and patience inherit the promises.

We will take note of one more phrase in there: "the powers of the age to come". We are not the focus of the Great Story that God is unfolding. Just as "they without us should not be made perfect" is said of the saints that preceded Jesus, we are preparing the scene for "the age to come". There is a tendency in every age to make our situation the end-all of God's plans. It is not. When Israel was set aside as unsuitable for faith and the "time of the nations" brought in, Israel whined, kicked, and resisted the Holy Spirit to the point of their own destruction. We too are approaching that point.

He uses this point to return to his subject. Here he picks up on his characterization of God's rest as a "promise" in 4:1. So it is important to realize that what he is talking about here is not some future promise of clouds and harps, but the present confidence of operating within the rest of God in the finished work of Christ. The other option we have is being "disapproved and near a curse; whose end is to be burned." It is also important to realize that the promise of God is our "hope set before" us now, which is a *present* anchor of the soul which encourages us *now* to enter "into what is within the veil". If this seems complicated to us, we can always grow up and chew our meat.

(6:13) For when God made promise to Abraham, since he had none greater to swear by, he swore by himself, saying,
> Surely blessing I will bless you,
> And multiplying I will multiply you.

And thus, having patiently endured, he obtained the promise. For men swear by the greater: and in every dispute of theirs the oath is final for confirmation. In which God, intending to show more abundantly to the heirs of the promise the immutability of his counsel, mediated with an oath; that by two immutable things, in which it is impossible for God to lie, we may have strong encouragement, who have fled for refuge to lay hold of the hope set before: which we have as the soul's anchor, both sure and firm and entering into what is within the veil; to where as forerunner Jesus entered for us, having become a high priest unto the age after the order of Melchizedek.

God said to Abraham (Genesis 22:16) "By myself I swear". Note that it is "heirs" of the promise, not "heir"; that is, this promise given to Abraham ("Because you do the word, even this, and keep not back your son, your only one, that to bless I bless you, and to increase I increase your seed as stars of the heavens and as sand which is on the sea shore; and he occupies—your seed—gate of ones hating him. And they bless themselves in your seed, all the nations of the earth, because you listen to my voice.") is linked with the promise of entering into God's rest. How so? The writer agrees with the point Paul makes in Galatians 3: "But to Abraham were the promises addressed, and to his seed: he does not say, And to seeds, as of many; but as of one, And to your seed; which is Christ." So we have *seed*, singular, and *heirs*, plural. Note also that God "mediated with an oath" and that section of Galatians goes on to say "a mediator is not of one, but God is one." Abraham's seed—Christ—has *become* the oath by which God mediated: "For the Son of God, Jesus Christ, he who was preached among you through us (through me and Silvanus and Timothy), did not become yes and no, but yes *is* in him. For whatever the promises of God, in him is the yes, and in him the amen".

And if God himself mediated with an oath, it is evident that he was not mediating between himself and man, as Christ now does, but between the one to whom the promise was delivered and the heirs of that promise. The writer will elaborate on this point in chapter nine; here we note that *once God could rest in the assurance of his work being finished, he could bring the blessing of Abraham to fruition in Abraham's seed and heirs because of the continuing priestly service of one from among them who had passed through the heavens*. Our connections with Abraham is by God's own oath; delivered by his Apostle Jesus, and serviced by the high priest he appointed to mediate between himself and us.

Having come this far, the writer can now delve into the subject of *what kind* of priesthood are we talking about by examining this "order of Melchizedek". First he compares Melchizedek to Abraham.

(7:1) For this Melchizedek, king of Salem, priest of the Most High God, who met Abraham returning from the slaughter of the kings and blessed him, to whom also Abraham divided a tenth of all (being first, by interpretation, King of righteousness, and then also King of Salem, which is, King of peace; fatherless, motherless, pedigree-less, having neither beginning of days nor end of life, but made like the Son of God), abides a priest continually. Now consider how great this one was to whom Abraham the patriarch gave a tenth out of the chief spoils. And they indeed of the sons of Levi that receive the priest's office have commandment to take tithes of the people according to the law, that is, of their brethren, though these have come out of the loin of Abraham: but he whose genealogy is not counted from them has tithed Abraham, and has blessed him that has the promises. But without any dispute the lesser is blessed of the greater. And here men that die receive tithes; but there one, of whom it is witnessed that he lives. And, so to speak, through Abraham Levi also, who receives tithes, has paid tithes; for he was yet in the loin of the father, when Melchizedek met him.

Next he compares the "order of Melchizedek" to the Levitical priesthood, and by proxy, the law.

(7:11) Now, therefore, if perfection was through the Levitical priesthood (for under it have the people received the law), what further need that another priest arise after the order of Melchizedek, and not be reckoned after the order of Aaron? For the priesthood being changed, of necessity a change is made also of law. For he of whom these *things* are said has partaken of another tribe, from which no one has given attendance at the altar. For it is evident that our Lord has sprung out of Judah; as to which tribe Moses spoke nothing concerning priests. And is yet more abundantly evident, if after the likeness of Melchizedek another priest arises who has been made, not after a law of carnal commandment, but after power of life indissoluble. For it is witnessed:

>You *are* priest unto the age
>After the order of Melchizedek.

The writer is barreling down a hill like a locomotive without brakes, and we have the luxury of pausing before moving on with him. This is a priesthood formed by "power of life indissoluble". This is more than just Christ interceding for us in a vague heavenly manner; this is *an entire order* of priesthood *which includes Melchizedek* and who knows who else. This is not merely 'doing away' with the law, but the continuing presence of a far more powerful law that operated before, *during*, and after Mosaic law. This cannot be relegated to the church age, sometimes called 'the day of grace'. This is not something that Christianity owns. It is far bigger than us; we are merely *"partakers* of the heavenly calling". In actual fact, we have very little idea who all was, is, and will be involved, as the writer later iterates in 13:23, "the universal gathering". Meanwhile the writer elaborates on the effect on Mosaic law of this order of priesthood being given its place publicly.

(7:18) For there is a disannulling of a foregoing commandment because of its weakness and unprofitableness (for the law made nothing perfect), and the introduction of a better hope, through which we draw near to God. And inasmuch as not without an oath (for they indeed have become priests without an oath; but he with an oath through him that says unto him,

> The Lord swore and will not repent himself,
> You: priest unto the age),

by so much also has Jesus become surety of a better covenant. And they indeed have become priests more in number, because that by death they are hindered from continuing on: but he, because he continues unto the age, has the priesthood unchangeable. Because of this also he is able to save to the uttermost them that approach God through him, he ever living to make intercession for them.

"Ever living" is the sense we get from this priestly order, whether we were aware that it existed or not. In this regard the writer's later comment, "Jesus Christ, the same, yesterday, today, and forever" is salient. Later we will get 'freshly slain and ever living".

One of the great subjects of Hebrews is the Eternal Covenant which the writer will be exploring later. However, where there is no guarantor for a covenant which God wishes to make, he uses an oath. Zacharias the father of John the Baptist made reference to the oath to Abraham, but other than that, only Hebrews mentions three distinct ones: God swearing that some would not enter his rest, God's swearing by himself to bless Abraham, and God's swearing an oath to establish Jesus as an eternal priest after the order of Melchizedek. The promises of God are well covered by Paul, but God's oaths are unique to Hebrews.

Having compared the Melchizedek priesthood to both Abraham and the Levitical priesthood, he summarizes with the qualifications of Jesus himself, emphasizing the qualities of true priesthood, as well as the fact that this particular oath came *after* the law was given, in contrast with Abraham's oath which was *before*.

(26) For such a high priest also became us, holy, guileless, undefiled, separated from sinners, and become higher than the heavens; who has no need daily, like the high priests, to offer up sacrifices, first for his own sins, and then for those of the people: for this he did once for all, when he offered up himself. For the law appoints high priests, men having infirmity; but the word of the oath which was after the law, Son, perfected unto the age.

At some point in this discussion the reality of what is being said is meant to sink in. and the reader ask, "What's the big deal with priesthood? Isn't the important thing that we're saved?" No, it is not. If God wishes to show us mercy and 'save' us, he is going to do it whether we like it or not. Ask Paul. But any fellowship, any growth, any moving forward, any accomplishments at all require that there be a high priest at the right hand of God preventing him from dropping an anvil on our heads when we deserve it, and preventing us from thinking that he's going to drop an anvil on our heads when we deserve it.

Now the writer starts his subject in earnest. If this priesthood is a larger reality than the reality which we have always known, *what else* is in that larger reality? What if everything we know is merely a *shadow* of an *image* of the real thing? How do we piece together the greater reality running everything from the little we know of the shadows? To address this he brings up the subject of the Covenant.

(8:1) Now a summary of the things of which we are speaking: We have such a high priest, who sat down on right hand of the throne of the Majesty in the heavens, a minister of the holies and

of the true tabernacle which the Lord pitched, not man. For every high priest is appointed to offer both gifts and sacrifices: thus it is necessary that this one also have something to offer. Now if he were on earth, he would not be a priest at all, there being those who offer the gifts according to law (the which serve a copy and shadow of the heavenlies, even as Moses when about to complete the tabernacle is warned: for,
    See,
says he,
    You make all according to the pattern shown you in the
        mount).
But now has he obtained a ministry the more superior, by so much as he is also mediator of a better covenant, which has been enacted upon better promises. For if that first had been faultless then would no place have been sought for a second. For blaming them he says,
    Lo, days come, says Lord,
    That I will accomplish a new covenant over the house of
        Israel and over the house of Judah;
    Not according to the covenant that I made for their fathers
    In day that I took them by their hand to lead them forth
        out of Egypt land:
    For they continued not in my covenant,
    And I regarded them not, says Lord.
    For this, the covenant, that I will covenant for the house of
        Israel after those days, says Lord;
    I will put my laws into their mind,
    And on their heart also will I write them:
    And I will be God to them,
    And they will be people to me:
    And they will each in no way teach his fellow citizen, and
        each his brother, saying, Know the Lord:
    For all will know me from least to greatest of them,

>   Because I will be merciful to their iniquities,
>   And their sins will I remember no more.
>
> In that he says, A new, he has made old the first. But what becomes old, yes aged, is near vanishing away.

This is remarkable. He begins by presenting the larger reality of "a high priest, who sat down on right hand of the throne of the Majesty in the heavens, a minister of the holies and of the true tabernacle which the Lord pitched, not man" *but then kindly for our sake* puts it into the context of physical things which we know about, both comparing and contrasting with the things with which we are familiar. He could have just said, "I'm going to tell you about an overriding reality that you know so little about that you might as well just bury your head in the sand," but that would hardly be a *priestly* approach. The tabernacle Moses built was *patterned* after the real one in the heavens. Did anyone *know* that there is a real one in the heavens? This news should have gone out like wildfire and ignited all kinds of investigations. What about David's design for the temple which he got from the Spirit which Solomon built? Is there a real temple in the heavens? What about the lesser temple that Ezra rebuilt? What about the one that Herod the Great built that Jesus cleaned out? What about Ezekiel's eight chapters of measurements for the new temple? Does the law of the leper have a heavenly correspondent? How about the vow of the Nazarite? How far does this go? What are the protocols and parameters of how to find out?

And more importantly, *do the things that we are doing today have a heavenly correspondent?* Perhaps something that we are completely unaware of. *But we do not have to be.* Here in the middle of Hebrews an entire realm of Christianity is opened up. The doors are flung wide open. Has anyone walked in? The silence is deafening. Perhaps that is why Jesus hinted that the stones themselves might speak up.

In all this, the focus is turned to a "new" covenant. And while we are tempted to say, "Oh yeah, that's the gospel," that is *not* how it is presented. The gospel is involved with entering into God's rest. This "new" covenant is involved with entering into the holies. It concerns the house—or household—of God as chapter ten says.

Meanwhile the writer is pointing out that it is the same law that is being set aside that provides the patterns and prophecies that point to the new thing that set it aside. In other words, there is no conflict. Mosaic law bows out gracefully, having done his full service. The *conflict* is from those who will not let go of the old even after it has bowed out. When God laid the cornerstone of the earth the morning stars sang together and all the sons of God shouted for joy. When God made the rock that the builders had rejected his chief cornerstone, all the sons of Israel gnashed their teeth and threw dust in the air.

Section II of Part III will deal with the Eternal Covenant which encompasses both the Apostleship (Part II) and Priesthood (first section of Part III). The writer will continue to compare and contrast the things with which we are already familiar with the things going on in the greater reality of heaven and God's counsels.

End of Section I of Part III

Takeaways:
- Purification of sins happens when someone becomes "in Christ".

- Propitiation for sins happens on a constant basis. It means getting someone who sympathizes with us, with whom God is pleased, close enough to God to intercede because God is pleased enough to listen.
- The qualifications to be an Intercessor (priest) are (1) to have taken full part in being human, and (2) to have "passed through the heavens" to demonstrate his suitability for the position. In other words, full earthly qualifications and full heavenly qualifications.
- The "perfecting' of Jesus was his complete full human life… including death.
- The "rest of God" is God resting from the work of reconciling man to himself, which work Jesus finished. There is more to God's rest: this is the part that applies to us.
- God's "promise" to Abraham and his seed (Jesus) could be fully implemented once God entered into his rest.
- Once God entered into his rest, he could start the new work of building his house and household, which is one of the subjects of the "promise".
- Building the house with Christ with confidence in God's promise is the "heavenly calling". It means participating in a reality larger than us.
- Things that God has put mankind through, such as giving them the law, were implemented to teach mankind that there is a larger reality than their own, and introduce them to it.
- Hebrews ranges through three of God's oaths before the writer shows that all of them are part of a larger agreement, the Eternal Covenant *into which all God's promises fit*.

Part III The Great High Priest
Section II   The Eternal Covenant
(*Section I of Part III was Melchizedek and the Law*)

(9:1) Now even the first had ordinances of service, and its worldly sanctuary. For a tabernacle was prepared, the first, in which are the candlestick, and the table, and the show-bread; which is called Holies. And after the second veil, the tabernacle called Holy of holies; having a golden altar of incense, and the ark of the covenant overlaid everywhere with gold in which is a golden pot holding the manna, and the rod of Aaron that budded, and the tables of the covenant; and above it cherubim of glory overshadowing the mercy-seat; of which one cannot now speak particularly. Now these having been thus prepared, the priests go in continually into the first tabernacle, accomplishing the services; but into the second the high priest alone once in the year, not without blood, which he offers for himself and for the ignorances of the people: the Holy Spirit signifying this, that the way into the holy place has not yet been made manifest, while the first tabernacle has standing; which is an image for the present season; according to which are offered both gifts and sacrifices that cannot, as to conscience, perfect the worshiper; only (with meats and drinks and diverse baptisms) carnal ordinances, imposed until a season of reformation.

The writer is plainly inviting us to discover for ourselves what the spiritual realities are for the candlestick, table, show-bread, the incense altar, the ark, the pot of manna, Aaron's rod, the tables of the covenant, and the cherubim of glory. He later tells us plainly (10:20) what, for example, the veil (Jesus' flesh) represents. He hints at what the tabernacle is but does not plainly spell it out. But to describe all these items in particular, then say there is not time now to speak about them, is to invite us to continue to explore what he presents. He mentions "season" twice; which is a much better word than 'dispensation'. Those who use the latter word attempt to categorize those in the various 'dispensations' as different kinds of people. We can, however, experience both winter and spring seasons without turning into something else.

(11) But Christ having come a high priest of the impending good, through the greater and more perfect tabernacle, not made with hands, that is, not of this creation, nor yet through blood of goats and calves, but by his own blood entered once for all into the holies, having obtained eternal redemption.

It helps us to pay attention to what is said about the heavenly reality itself, and what is being described in terms of the earthly representations of heaven. The writer uses both freely, yet keeps them distinct. At times he compares them and at times he contrasts them. A great deal of confusion can be garnered by contrasting where he compares, and comparing where he contrasts, obligating Christ to do all sorts of things that have nothing to do with the heavenly reality and everything to do with the earthly. Some things were necessary in the law because the law was on earth (such as new priests taking over for priests who died) and have no counterpart in heaven. Some things were necessary in the law because we needed exact representations of the things in heaven, as listed at the beginning of the chapter. And some things were necessary in the law to point out the limitations of the law itself and invite us to ask God what is next. In this respect, he says "high priest of the impending good", inviting us to explore what we have not yet been told.

The previous section is speaking of heaven and contrasting it with this physical creation. As he continues, he gives the effect of this heavenly event on we who are still living on earth.

(13) For if the blood of goats and bulls, and ashes of a heifer sprinkling the defiled, sanctify unto the cleanness of the flesh: how much more will the blood of the Christ, who through Eternal Spirit offered himself without blemish to the God, clean our conscience from dead works to serve Living God?

Note that those who are still expecting a gospel tract here would have wanted it to say "clean us from all sins so that we can be saved". But it simply says "clean our conscience from dead works to serve Living God". John gives us cleaning from sin and from unrighteousness, Paul gives us purifying ourselves from every pollution of flesh and spirit, James tells us to purify our hearts and Peter tells us of purifying our souls. All of these processes happen *after* we are saved. The only washing or cleaning that happens in the salvation process is done by the Spirit, not us (First Corinthians 6:11). A clean conscience is healthy and strong; we can not serve a Living God we are concerned with other things that we 'should' be doing.

Note also that he did not offer his blood; he offered *himself* and shed his blood in the process. Note also that as the introduction of the heavenly reality unfolds, more and more of what is "Eternal" is exposed. As such, when he talks about both 'new covenant' and the 'first covenant' below, he is constrained to say what the nature of a Covenant is in the *eternal* sense, which applies in *all* cases on earth or in heaven.

(15) And because of this he is New Covenant Mediator, so that a death having taken place for redemption of the transgressions under the first covenant, the called may receive the promise of the eternal inheritance.

And he begins to show that the 'oath' by which he swore to Abraham—as well as the other two oaths—were not incidental whims of God's but part of a much more intricate transaction in which there is:
- The Covenant. This is the agreement to give earned value for ownership of a desired item.
- The Covenant Maker. This is the one who sets the values and oversees the exchange.
- The Covenant Guarantor. This is the testator who gives the earned value.
- The Covenant Seller. This is the one who gets the earned value and gives the desired item.
- The Covenant Inheritor. This is the one who gets the desired item; the Beneficiary.
- The Covenant Value. This is the 'earned value' which is given to the Covenant Seller.
- The Covenant Transaction. This is when the Covenant Maker declares satisfaction of the Covenant by proper transfer of Value from Guarantor to Seller, at which point the Inheritor receives his inheritance.

The "death" of the next section refers to the death of Guarantor's ownership of the Value. The writer uses a last will and testament to illustrate this. In both a 'will' and in the case of Christ purchasing us (redemption), it is *life* which is the Earned Value which is given up for the benefit of the Inheritor, at which point the inheritance—the promises of God as to a new covenant relationship—are passed to the Beneficiaries—Christ resurrected and his companions. The Covenant Seller in this transaction is the Law, and satisfaction of the Covenant Transaction was Jesus death that prevented his claiming the life promised by the law. *This* covenant is sketched out here briefly to show that (1) the protocols are exacting and specific, and (2) the writer of

Hebrews knew them well enough to responsibly be discussing the one covenant that supersedes and generates all others.

(17) For where a covenant is, death necessarily is brought in of the covenanted. For a covenant is on the dead confirmed since it is not effective while the covenanted lives.

The writer then explains what so many onlookers to the ritual of sacrificing animals have wondered: is God thirsty for blood, or why does he require these constant sacrifices?

(18) Thus even the first has not been dedicated without blood. For when every commandment had been spoken by Moses to the whole people according to the law, he took the blood of the calves and the goats, with water and scarlet wool and hyssop, sprinkled both the book itself and the whole people, saying,
> This—the blood of the covenant which the God commands toward you.

Moreover the tabernacle and all the vessels of the ministry he sprinkled likewise with the blood. And according to the law, almost all things are cleaned with blood, and apart from shedding of blood is no pardon.

Jesus' lifeblood as the Covenant Value ('money' in lesser covenants like Abraham buying Sarah's tomb) is the theme which God set as the border between the physical creation and the "impending good". We note that the writer of Hebrews is speaking of the Eternal Covenant here but not sketching out the full terms. It is, in fact, too large for mortals to easily comprehend, as are the full implications of Paul's 'mystery'. However, he does give us the parts that apply to our joining with Christ and serving God, while providing enough hints to facilitate discovery.

And those of us who define impending good as 'getting rid of the bad' will now be told that the *heavens* are *also* getting "cleaned" for this impending good. Now it makes sense why 'cleaned' is from dead works to serve Living God. It is not just we humans who enter into the good of the Rest of God. What an angel was doing *before* Jesus "passed through the heavens" as a man, is different from what that same angel would be doing *after*.

(23) It was necessary therefore that the copies of the heavenlies be cleaned with these; but the heavenlies themselves with better sacrifices than these. For Christ entered not into holies made with hands, antitypes of the true; but into the very heaven, now to appear before the face of the God for us. Nor yet that he offer himself often, as the high priest enters into the holies yearly with blood not his own; else must he often have suffered since the world's foundation. But now once, at conclusion of the ages, he has been manifested to put away the sin by the sacrifice of himself. And inasmuch as it is laid up for the men once to die, and after this—judgment; thus also the Christ, having been once offered to bear sins of many, secondly without sin will appear to the ones awaiting him into salvation.

Again, we break here to note that "conclusion of the ages" is just that. Heavenly ages, earthly ages, things present, things past, things to come—all of them. They all are concluded with the transaction of Christ giving up his mortal life. All events conclude with that event. Later this will be succinctly reiterated: "Jesus Christ the same, yesterday, today, and forever." The Chief Cornerstone is the chief cornerstone of *everything* in every age. The only thing outside the ages is God.

The writer pens his finishing salvo in full style. He has saved his most powerful point for last, and he does not even attempt to make it himself—he allows Scripture to speak. The subject he has been waiting to introduce is not the place of angels, not the rest of God, not the heavenly realities, but *one particular body*.

(10:1) For the law having a shadow of the impending good, not the very image of the things, they can never with the same yearly sacrifices which they offer continually make perfect them that draw near. Else would they not have ceased to be offered, because the worshiper having been once cleaned would have had no more consciousness of sins? But in these, yearly remembrance of sins. For it is impossible for blood of bulls and goats to take away sins. For which reason when he comes into the world, he says,

> Sacrifice and offering you would not,
> But a body did you prepare me;
> In burnt offerings and about sin you delight not:
> Then said I, Lo, I am come
> (In summary of book it has been written of me)
> To do your will, O God.

The writer has made his point. We now have the two most disparate elements in existence working together: the eternal will of God and a mortal human body. He could lay his pen down now, but considering our condition, would hardly be *priestly*. So he reiterates.

(8) Above saying:
> Sacrifices and offerings and burnt offerings and about sin
> You do not will,
> Nor yet you delight,

which according to the law are offered. Then he has declared,

> Lo, I come to do your will.

He takes away the first, that he may establish the second. By which will we have been sanctified through the offering of the body of Jesus Christ once for all.

The finality of these words are belied by the writer's patient continuance. He has the point, he has written the point down, but he is quite aware that we are capable of reading the point without noticing. For the rest of the book he will be winding down. But the very fact that he is still writing impels him to continue to open new doors to new realms in the hopes that we will enter them.

(11) And every priest indeed stands daily ministering and offering often the same sacrifices, the which can never take away sins; but this, when he had offered one sacrifice for sins for ever, sat down at God's right: from here on expecting until his enemies be made footstool of his feet. For by one offering he has perfected for ever those being sanctified.

Now consider what is being said here. The word "one" and the word "forever" do not often occur together; here they do twice. There is *one* sacrifice for sins *for ever*. All failure—everywhere—goes back to that one sacrifice for inspection. The world was made *for* him… and is inspected by his guarantee to God that it would be pleasing. God did not declare the second day good. This comes to the cross for inspection. The heavens that divided the waters from the waters stand before the man who can declare them good or discard them. Cain killed Abel. They come to the cross for inspection and stand before the man that can declare them good or reject them. We go to God to present ourselves. And just as God did with Satan: "Why are you coming to me? Go to Job and test your opinion of man", God says to us, "Go to

Christ on the cross and see what he says. If he will take you, I will." "But I say to you, my friends, Fear not those who kill the body and after this have no more that they can do. But I will warn you whom you will fear: Fear *him* who after he has killed has authority to cast into hell; yes, I say to you, Fear *him*."

And "by *one* offering he has perfected *for ever* (into the finality) those being sanctified". Note that the process of being *sanctified* is ongoing, but the *perfection* was done once by one act. The emphasis on the finality of finishing God's work could not be stronger. Having made this point as strong as he could make it for us to hear, he moves on to those elements that have to do with our "being sanctified".

(15) And the Holy Spirit also bears witness to us; for after the former declaration,
> This *is* the covenant that I will be covenanting toward them,
> After those, the days, says the Lord:
> Giving my laws on their hearts,
> And on their minds will I write them;
> And their sins and their iniquities, no, I will be reminded no more.

Now where there is pardon of these, there is no more offering for sin.

End of Section II of Part III
(End of Part III)

Takeaways:
- The heavenly reality can be understood by looking at the earthly laws that God had given.
- The Eternal Covenant is huge, but we are clearly told about the part that applies to us.
- Every transaction of man from us buying flashlight batteries to Christ redeeming those under law is a covenant and follows the protocols of the Eternal Covenant.
- Because the death of Christ's mortal life is the pivot of the Eternal Covenant, God insists that all transactions include recognition of this fact, whether we consciously realize why or not.
- The "Rest of God" is what allows the universe to continue, and was accomplished in a human body.
- The "will of God" has been validated by his creation, specifically Jesus' life, and having been validated, can unfold into the "impending good" that he has been waiting to bring.
- Now that we know this, the writer can tell us specifically what to do about it.

Part IV Who Is Coming Along, and Where Are We Going?

Before he gets to the Path of Faith and its peculiar topography, he picks out a few points to make, that at first blush seem of little consequence. But they are all based on the little flash of insight he gives regarding a heavenly reality; that the veil of the heavenly tabernacle which guarded the most holy place was in fact, Jesus' flesh. This one clue allows us to piece together the rest of the heavenly reality without him having to spend several more chapters explaining things "of which one cannot now speak particularly". The first line regarding the "freshly killed—and [always] living—way" shows the vastly different ideas that are joined together in our journey to God. This is the same word for "freshly killed" as the lamb in Revelation five. "A new and living way" does not express it. Likewise, as mentioned in 8:13 where he also quoted the same passage from Jeremiah above, "house" also means "household" over which this "great priest" is presiding. In other words, this path is both individual and *social*, so his first 'instructions' here are in reference to how we wash "the body" (singular) of God's household with "clean water" (the word) by first having our "hearts" (plural) "sprinkled" (with the freshly killed blood) "from an evil conscience" (willfully sinning) with the view of the "impending good", here phrased "as you see the day drawing near".

(10:19) Having therefore, brethren, boldness to enter into the holies by the blood of Jesus, by freshly killed—and living—way, which he dedicated for us through the veil, that is, his flesh; and having a great priest over the house of God; let us approach with true heart in full assurance of faith, having the hearts sprinkled from an evil conscience: and having the body washed in clean water. Let us hold fast the unwavering confession of the hope, for faithful he that promised. And let us consider one another unto provoking of love and good works; not forsaking the assembling of ourselves together, as is a custom of some, but exhorting; and so much the more, as you see the day drawing near.

This path of faith is for those who have entered God's rest—note that labels such as 'saved' and 'unsaved' are of little use in Hebrews—and are ready to approach God. Where does it lead? Abraham "went out, not knowing to where he was going." But the writer can round out the picture a bit more for us as he will in chapter twelve. First he must contrast the confidence of faith with the false confidence of sinning willfully, which he will also detail in chapter twelve as (1) falling short of the grace of God, (2) having a root of bitterness, and (3) being a profane person. These are different than from merely disbelieving and not entering God's rest: this is the failing of those who profess to have entered God's rest, but are not "united by faith" with Jesus and as a result find themselves in more condemnation than if they had not "known the way of righteousness" as Peter says. This is God judging "his people".

(10:26) For if we sin willfully after we have received the knowledge of the truth, no more sacrifice remains for sins, but a certain fearful expectation of judgment, and a fierceness of fire which will devour the adversaries. One that has set at nothing Moses' law dies without compassion on two or three witnesses. Of how much sorer punishment, think you, will he be judged worthy who has trodden under the Son of God, and has deemed the blood of the covenant with which he was sanctified common, and has insulted the Spirit of Grace? For we know him that said,
     Vengeance is mine, I will repay.
And again,
     The Lord will judge his people.

Fearful, the falling into Living God's hands.

"Trodden under" is considering our wants to be of more immediate consequence than the Son of God's wants. Deeming his blood "common" (or 'contaminating') is being embarrassed or ashamed of God's acceptance of such a puerile manner of approaching him. Outraging (insulting) the "Spirit of Grace" is using his gifts to benefit ourselves rather than the household of God. These are not 'bad things to do that we should avoid', these are absolute disqualifications from belonging to the household of God.

And the writer knows that we all can tend toward these attitudes. So just as in the warnings of chapter six, he points out the fruit that has been evidenced so far, and focuses us on patience, confidence, and boldness.

(32) But call to remembrance the former days in which, after you were enlightened, you endured a great conflict of sufferings: partly being made a gazing-stock both by reproaches and afflictions; and partly becoming partakers with them that were so used. For you both sympathized with those in bonds, and took joyfully the spoiling of your possessions, knowing that you have yourselves possession better and abiding. Cast not away therefore your confidence, which has great recompense of reward. For you have need of patience, that, having done the will of God, you may receive the promise.
> For yet a little, as long as it is as long as,
> The one coming will be arriving and will not be delaying;
> But my righteous one will live from faith:
> And if he draw back, my soul has no pleasure in him.

But we are not of them that draw back unto destruction; but of faith into procuring of soul.

Having directed us to the Path of Faith, and having taken us into the holiest of holies in God's real temple in the real heavens and given us a push, he can now describe for us this path. And this path did not start at Pentecost, nor with Moses, nor even with Abraham and the Patriarchs. This path goes all the way back to the beginning of mankind. Those of us who wish all our troubles to be solved by the "one coming" (as were Adam and Eve; they too were looking for the 'woman's seed' which would bruise Satan's head) forget that we are called to *participate* with what he is doing, right now, right where we are.

The path begins with us acting on the fact that there is more to life than what we see or what we think we know. By definition, *God himself* is more than we *can* see or know. When we put ourselves in this position of vulnerability—that of *not* knowing—we have started the path of faith. Job's friends missed that path of not knowing; even the last comment tolerated by Job which Bildad made tries to attribute unknown elements to God, but falls short of "We simply do not know" which is a very intelligent thing to say. When we *don't know* and go forward anyway, it means that we believe in a God who made things with purpose, provision, and kindness. When we don't know and *stop*, it means that our confidence is solely rooted in ourselves and we do not believe God can be trusted.

When we say, "I will work with you on this, my God" he notices. When God notices something, there is a change in its very state of existence, because he does not look on sin. When God notices someone, every spiritual being also takes note of that person. For our part, the Path of Faith starts with not knowing yet going forward. For God's part, our Path of Faith starts with him taking note: this is called *witness*, which he will bring up again at the conclusion of the chapter.

(11:1) Now faith is assurance of things hoped for, conviction of things unseen, for in it the elders had witness borne them. By faith we understand that the ages have been framed by God's word, so that what is seen has not been made out of things which appear. By faith Abel offered unto the God a sacrifice superior to Cain's, through which he had witness borne that he was righteous, the God bearing witness over his gifts: and through it he being dead yet speaks. By faith Enoch was translated that he should not see death; and he was not found, because the God translated him; for he has had witness borne him before the translation that he had been well-pleasing to the God.

The writer now introduces the second part of the Path of Faith; the expectation that God will draw near to us when we draw near to him; that there is *benefit* to approaching him.

(6) But without faith it is impossible to be well-pleasing; for who comes to the God must believe that he is, and is rewarder of them that seek after him.

Now the writer brings in a much-needed element; the fact that this *benefit* (reward) of drawing near to God, *by definition*, does not fully manifest during our lifetime because God is larger than our lifetime, and "if in this life only we have hope in Christ, we are most miserable of all men." And a corollary of this is that we will receive *something* during our lifetime that will give us the necessary "assurance of things hoped for" to strengthen the "conviction of things unseen". This brings up the subjects of God's promises and our inheritance.

(7) By faith Noah, warned concerning the things not seen as yet,

with godly fear prepared an ark to saving of his house; through which he condemned the world and became (according to faith) heir of the righteousness. By faith Abraham, when called, obeyed to go out unto a place which he was to receive for inheritance, and went out, not knowing to where he was going. By faith he became sojourner in land of the promise, as foreign-placed, dwelling in tents with Isaac and Jacob, the fellow-heirs of the same promise. For he awaited the city which has the foundations, whose builder and maker is the God. By faith Sarah herself received power to conceive seed even when past season of prime, since she counted him faithful who had promised. For which reason also from one were begotten, and him as good as dead, even

> As the stars of the heaven in multitude,
> And as the sand, which is by the shore of the sea, the unnumbered.

These all died according to faith, not having received the promises, but having seen them and greeted from afar, and having confessed that they were strangers and pilgrims on the earth.

He has just iterated the next point of the path of faith: if our hope is in the promise of God for an inheritance we are not getting in this life, then the elements of this life provide an insufficient reality for our desires. This leads us to the realization that (1) our desires, being larger than this life, actually lead *toward* God and do not need to be used up on our lusts, and (2) God has *prepared* the answer to our desires, and we can join him in that *preparation* with what we do now.

(14) The ones saying such are manifesting that Fatherland they are seeking. And if indeed they had minded that from which they went out, they would have had opportunity to return. But now

they desire a better, that is, a heavenly: for which reason the God is not ashamed of them, to be called their God; for he has prepared them a city. By faith Abraham, being tried, has offered up the Isaac, and who had gladly received the promises was offering up his only begotten; toward whom it was spoken,

> In Isaac shall your seed be called:

reckoning that also out of dead God is able to raise up, from where also in a parable he recovers. By faith Isaac blessed the Jacob and the Esau, even concerning things to come. By faith Jacob dying blessed each of the sons of Joseph and worshipped on the top of his staff. By faith Joseph, dying, remembers the exodus of the sons of Israel; and directs concerning his bones.

Now he introduces a new element: our rejection of the limitations of this world.

(23) By faith, Moses being born, was hid three months by his fathers because they saw the child capable; and they were not afraid of the commandment of the king. By faith Moses, become great, refused to be called son of Pharaoh's daughter; choosing rather to share ill treatment with the people of the God, than to enjoy sin for a season; deeming greater riches than the treasures of Egypt the reproach of the Christ, for he looked unto the recompense of reward. By faith he forsook Egypt, not fearing the fury of the king: for he endured, as seeing him who is invisible. By faith he instituted the passover and the sprinkling of the blood, that the destroyer of the firstborn should not touch them. By faith they passed through the Red Sea as by dry land: which the Egyptians attempting to do were swallowed up. By faith the walls of Jericho fell down, being surrounded for seven days. By faith Raab the harlot perished not with the disbelieving, having received the spies with peace.

The amount of detail and teaching he packs into these examples is staggering; fortunately we need only to focus on his larger point. He now hits up the *accomplishments* of the path of faith:

(32) And what more may I be saying? For the time will fail me if I tell of Gideon, Barak, Sampson, Jephtha; and of David and Samuel and the prophets: who through faith subdued kingdoms, wrought righteousness, obtained promises, stopped lions' mouths, quenched fire's power, escaped sword's edge, from weakness were made strong, waxed mighty in war, routed armies of aliens. Women received their dead by resurrection.

And the final element is the rejection of anything that would deviate us from the Path of Faith once we have embarked on it.

(36) Yet others were tortured, not accepting the deliverance, that they might obtain a better resurrection. And others had trial of mockings and scourgings, yes, moreover of bonds and imprisonment. They were stoned, were tempted, sawn apart, died by sword's slaughter; went about in sheepskins, in goatskins; destitute, afflicted, ill-treated (of whom the world was not worthy), wandering in deserts and mountains and caves, and the holes of the earth.

Having laid out the history of the witnesses in scripture according to a peculiar pattern of which one cannot now speak particularly, he brings the point back home to "Let us hold fast the unwavering confession of the hope, for faithful he that promised."

(39) And these all, witnessed to through the faith, received not the promise, the God having foreseen something better concerning us, that apart from us they be not made perfect.

This last phrase is loaded. What is it that *we* are doing which is so necessary to *them*? They looked for a city that they have not yet received the same as us, as he will point out in the last chapter. Everything *looks* the same for them and for us. Their use of faith is not differentiated from our use of faith. What is "something better"? Very simply, it is the revealing of the Apostle and High Priest of our confession: Jesus, or as he will say shortly, "Jesus the Author and Perfecter of the faith." In all these ages he just described, people had been wondering just what the crux of being created humans was going to turn out to be. Moses *really* lamented this in his psalm, and ends with a cry for our works to be somehow meaningful. The writer of Hebrews has pointed out that the answer to the crux of being human is found in the body of Jesus, with everything that his living in that body entailed.

We have not yet received the "unshakable kingdom" but we can intelligently walk into the holies with boldness and present our requests to God himself. This is necessary to those who lived before Jesus because we are engaged in the same duality that the Son of God has shown us. He lived on earth then "passed through the heavens" and by him we have access to the heavens while living on earth. Before Jesus, we did not. It is necessary to have humans whom he calls "brothers" using Jesus' boldness *while in mortal bodies like he had* and like those with faith in past times had. Why? because this justifies God.

How? "Whom God has set forth as propitiation through faith in his blood to show his righteousness, because of the passing over of the sins done before through the forbearance of God: for showing of his righteousness in the present time, that *he* might be just, and justify him that is of faith of Jesus." If the common element between us and Joab were levels of revelation, Joab would lose out. But if it is faith, we are on equal ground. Today God is demonstrating that it is righteous for him to listen to Christ's intercession and put up with our weaknesses, as well as "passing over of the sins done before" by those who lived before Christ came. If Jesus had taken all his own directly to heaven instead of leaving them on earth with the promised Holy Spirit, the current demonstration of God's grace would not be occurring, and the 'perfecting' (finishing) of his own in past times would be left dangling as if the promises were never meant to have effect in this lifetime, or for mortals. But they were promised to mortals. And any blessings that *can* be enjoyed by mortality are now available to us.

But we are grafted into this tree of the faith of the fathers, not they into us; we bear the fruit but they provide the root. Without them we have no promises to be brought into, and without us they have no demonstration of God fulfilling his promises in season. Each age justifies God in a different manner, yet they all work together. God uses a flood to end one age, and the Son of Man to end another.

This point is necessary if we are to understand both the contrasts and commonalities we share with 'Old Testament saints' and for that matter 'millennium saints'. Some prophecies must be fulfilled before others. The Son of Man was to suffer, *then* enter into his glory. Many of the prophecies are literally fulfilled in us, though we might wonder about Peter quoting that the sun would be changed into darkness and the moon into blood. And many are not. It is a complex story that requires us to *go on together* (without false distinctions) to see how it will play out. "Boast not against the branches; but if you boast, *you* do not bear the root, but the root you." We are all offspring of God as Paul says, and the Spirit of Christ has been, and will continue to be, operative in men since the beginning.

Before he can finish the question of 'Who is coming along, and where are we going?' he must distinguish between discipline and disapproval.

(12:1) Therefore now we also, having so great a cloud of witnesses encompassing us, let us lay aside every weight and the easily besetting sin, through endurance let us run the race set before us; looking unto the Author and Perfecter of the faith, Jesus, who for the joy set before him endured a cross, despising shame, and has sat down at the right of the throne of the God.

It is a race. Paul says "Know you not that they who run in the stadium all run, but *one* receives the prize? Thus run in order that you may obtain. But every one that contends is self-controlling in all things: *they* then indeed that they may receive a corruptible crown, but *we* an incorruptible. *I* therefore thus am racing, not as uncertainly; so I box, not as punching the air; but I push my body and lead it captive, lest having preached to others I should myself be disqualified." And there are rules. "And if also if one compete, he is not crowned except he compete lawfully." And we can win. "I have fought the good fight, I have finished the race, I have kept the faith. Furthermore the crown of righteousness is laid up for me, which the Lord, the righteous Judge, will give to me in that day; but not only to me, but also to all who love his appearing." So who are we competing with? "But I have labored more abundantly than they all, but not I, but the grace of the God with me." Yet it is the *prize*, not the competition that motivates; "but one thing—forgetting the things behind, and stretching out those before, I pursue towards the mark, unto the prize of the calling on high of the God in Christ

Jesus", just as Jesus "who for the joy set before him endured a cross, despising the shame". There is a race with rules and prizes for the winners. And we thought we were just here to praise God.

The dichotomy he introduces next is peculiar. We get exhausted by the race because we have forgotten about how Jesus operated. Then we get prodded by God to keep moving, and think we have done something wrong, and faint in our minds instead of waking up and realizing that God keeps us on course because we are his sons. The writer takes the time to establish the practical reality of being related to God.

(3) For consider him that has endured such contradiction of sinners against himself that you weary not, fainting in your souls. You have not yet resisted unto blood, striving against the sin: and have forgotten the exhortation which reasons with you as with sons,

>My son, regard not lightly the Lord's chastening,
>Nor faint when reproved of him;
>For whom the Lord loves he chastens,
>And scourges every son whom he receives.

For chastening you endure; the God deals with you as with sons. For who is the son whom a father chastens not? But if you are without chastening, of which all have been made partakers, then are you bastards, and not sons. Furthermore, we had the fathers of our flesh as chasteners, and we reverenced; shall we not much rather be subject to the Father of the spirits, and live? For they indeed for a few days chastened as seemed good to them; but he for the profit, for the partaking of his holiness. Now all chastening seems for the present to be not joyous but grievous; yet afterward yields to those exercised by it peaceable fruit of righteousness.

His *description*, however, of the condition we find ourselves in is somewhat more dramatic.

(13) For this reason straighten the hanging down hands, and the paralyzed knees, and make straight paths for your feet, that what is lame be not turned aside, but rather may be healed.

The first time he *seemed* to be giving random instructions was in 10:24, and they led right into his warnings against willfully sinning. Here he provides another disarming instruction—to follow after peace with all—coupling it with sanctification, which seems to be a complete non-sequitur until we remember that it has been used consistently so far for our association with Jesus by his blood; which association also puts us in a company of people with whom there must be peace to continue on. And as before, he leads right into warnings against those who contaminate sanctification.

(14) Follow after peace with all, and the sanctification without which no one will see the Lord: looking carefully lest any be falling short of the grace of the God; lest any root of bitterness springing up trouble, and through this the many be defiled; lest any fornicator, or profane, as Esau, who for one meal sold his own birthright. For you know that even when he afterward desired to inherit the blessing, he was disapproved; for he found no place for repentance, though he sought it diligently with tears.

These three breaks from the path that Jesus blazed for us are the final state of any "who has trodden under the Son of God, and has deemed the blood of the covenant with which he was sanctified common, and has insulted the Spirit of Grace" that the writer mentioned in 10:26, which were again a result of what he mentioned in 6:4: "those who were once enlightened and tasted of the heavenly gift, and became partakers of Holy Spirit, and tasted the good word of God, and the powers of the age to come, and fell away, it is impossible to renew again unto repentance; they crucifying again to themselves and openly shaming the Son of God." *None* of these show "godly fear and awe"; indeed, those who break from the path are often the most charismatic and confident in the assembly, identified only by their dismissive attitude toward holiness (being set apart by the sprinkling of Jesus' blood) and lack of real fruit. We need to be "looking carefully" because they gravitate toward leadership positions.

A note on 'sprinkling'; our culture has lost the sense of this word. The tattoo of a member of a biker gang is his 'colors'; it proves his association. In wartime it is vital to be able to be immediately identified with the flag under which one operates. This *association with a greater power to which one is allied* is what is meant by 'sprinkling'; it is not just a ritual. In the Old testament 'sprinkling' has the sense of bestowing the favor of allowing someone to carry the name and cause of a dignitary. The 'blood of sprinkling' in Hebrews means that we are *associated* personally, publicly, and before God with Jesus. Thus the *faith of Jesus* is more than just having faith in him, it is being associated with his very life. The ramifications are many, and the penalties for violating one's allegiance are far more severe than merely doing something to upset a dignitary. If he allows us to carry his flag, we stand for everything that flag stands for.

(18) For you are not come to a palpable burning fire, and to blackness, and darkness, and tempest, and sound of a trumpet, and voice of words which they that heard entreated that no word be added for them. For they could not endure what was enjoined:
    If even a beast impinge on the mountain it will be stoned.

And so fearful was the appearance Moses said,
> I exceedingly fear and quake.

But you are come unto mount Zion; and unto city of living God, heavenly Jerusalem; and to myriads of angels; to universal assembly; and to church of firstborns enrolled in heavens; and to God, judge of all; and to spirits of just ones perfected; and new covenant mediator, Jesus; and blood of sprinkling speaking better than the Abel.

Um… wow? If there is a solid bridge between Paul's 'mystery' and the book of Revelation, this is it. Let us take a moment and put together those two revelations using those nine aspects of our destination. The comparison is a veritable recipe-book for understanding God's handling of the seasons.

Mount Zion
- For I do not wish you to be ignorant, brothers, of this mystery, that you may not be wise in your own conceits, that blindness in part is happened to Israel, until the fullness of the nations be come in; and so all Israel shall be saved. According as it is written, The deliverer shall come out of Zion; he shall turn away ungodliness from Jacob.
- And I saw, and behold, the Lamb standing upon mount Zion, and with him a hundred forty-four thousand, having his name and the name of his Father written upon their foreheads.

City of the Living God, heavenly Jerusalem
- For Hagar is mount Sinai in Arabia, and corresponds to Jerusalem which is now, for she is in bondage with her children, but the

Jerusalem above is free, which is our mother. For it is written, Rejoice, you barren that bear not; break out and cry, you that travail not; because the children of the desolate are more numerous than of her that has a husband.
- He that overcomes, him will I make a pillar in the temple of my God and he shall go no more at all out. And I will write upon him the name of my God, and the name of the city of my God: the new Jerusalem which comes down out of heaven from my God, and my new name.

Myriads of angels
- And to you that are troubled repose with us, at the revelation of the Lord Jesus from heaven, with angels of his power, in flaming fire taking vengeance on those who know not God and those who do not obey the glad tidings of our Lord Jesus Christ; who shall pay the penalty: everlasting destruction from presence of the Lord, and from the glory of his might when he will have come to be glorified in his saints, and wondered at in all that have believed (for our testimony to you has been believed) in that day.
- And they sing a new song, saying, You are worthy to take the book, and to open its seals because you have been slain, and have redeemed to God by your blood out of every tribe, and tongue, and people, and nation; and made them to our God kings and priests; and they will reign over the earth. And I saw, and I heard voice of many angels around the throne and the living creatures and the elders; and their

number was ten thousands of ten thousands and thousands of thousands; saying with a loud voice, Worthy is the Lamb that has been slain, to receive power, and riches, and wisdom, and strength, and honour, and glory, and blessing.

Universal assembly
- The Father of whom every family in heavens and on earth is named
- After these things I saw, and lo, a great crowd which no one could number, out of every nation and tribes and peoples and tongues standing before the throne and before the Lamb, clothed with white robes and palm branches in their hands.

Church of firstborns enrolled in heavens
- For if the casting away of them is a reconciling of a world, what is the receiving but life from dead? And if the first-fruit holy, the lump also; and if the root holy, the branches also.
- These are they who follow the Lamb wheresoever it goes. These have been bought from men; first-fruits to God and to the Lamb: and in their mouths was no lie found: they are blameless.

God, judge of all
- What then the superiority of the Jew? or what the profit of circumcision? Much every way: and first, indeed, that to them were entrusted the oracles of God. For what? if some have not believed, will their unbelief make the faith of

God of none effect? Far be the thought: but let God be true, and every man false; according as it is written, So that you should be justified in your words, and should overcome when you are in judgment. But if our unrighteousness commend God's righteousness, what shall we say? Is God unrighteous who inflicts wrath? I speak according to man. Far be the thought: since how shall God judge the world?

- And the twenty-four elders, who sit on their thrones before God, fell upon their faces, and worshipped God saying, We give you thanks, Lord God Almighty, who is, and who was, that you have taken your great power and have reigned. And the nations have been full of wrath, and your wrath is come and the time of the dead to be judged; and to give the reward to your servants the prophets and to the saints and to those who fear your name, small and great; and to destroy those that destroy the earth.

Spirits of just ones perfected:
- For the perfecting of the saints; with a view to work of ministry; with a view to the edifying of the body of Christ until we all arrive at the unity of the faith and of the knowledge of the Son of God, at full-grown man, at measure of the stature of the fullness of the Christ.
- And he said to me, These words: faithful and true. And the Lord God of the spirits of the prophets has sent his angel to shew to his bondmen the things which must soon come to pass.

New covenant mediator, Jesus

- For this is good and acceptable before our Saviour God who desires that all men should be saved and come to knowledge of truth. For one, God: also one is mediator between God and men, a man, Christ Jesus, who gave himself a ransom for all, the testimony for its own times.
- I Jesus have sent mine angel to testify these things to you in the assemblies. I am the root and offspring of David, the bright, morning star.

Blood of sprinkling speaking better things than the Abel

- That you were at that season without Christ, aliens from the commonwealth of Israel, and strangers to the covenants of the promise, having no hope, and without God in the world, but now in Christ Jesus *you* who once were far off are become near by the blood of the Christ. For *he* is our peace, who has made both one, and has broken down the middle wall of the partition.
- And one of the elders answered, saying to me, These arrayed in the white robes, who are they, and from where came they? And I said to him, My lord, *you* know. And he spoke to me, These are they that come out of the great tribulation, and they washed their robes, and made them white in the blood of the Lamb. Therefore are they before the throne of the God and serve him day and night in his temple: and who sits on the throne will tabernacle over them. They will hunger no more, nor thirst any more;

> neither will the sun strike upon them, nor any heat because the Lamb that is amid the throne will shepherd them, and guide them unto fountains of waters of life: and the God will wipe away every tear from their eyes.

It is remarkable how well the writer weaves our intimate relationship with God and each other together with formal respect. There is no couching his words in 'Jesus is nice' language. Jesus may very well be kind, but we are dealing with an Eternal God who does not put up with indolence.

(25) See you refuse not him that speaks. For if *they* escaped not when they refused him that warned on earth, much less we who turn away from him that is from heavens, whose voice then shook the earth but now he has promised, saying,
> Yet once more will I make to tremble not the earth only,
> But also the heaven.

And this, Yet once more, signifies the removing of the shaken, as of things made, that those not shaken may remain. For this reason, receiving an unshakable kingdom, let us have grace, by which we may offer service well-pleasing to the God with godly fear and awe; for our God is indeed a consuming fire.

"Let us have grace"? That is a strange way to face off with a voice that is shaking both the earth and the heavens to the extent of their complete removal. 'Grace' is unshakable because it is not "made" but given; and apparently nonflammable.

For the third time the writer delves into instructions. If either of the two previous examples taught us anything, he is going to use this to make a point he has been holding back for some time. In this case he inserts it innocuously into the middle without explanation. We have quoted it several times throughout this paper, and it is the single most concentrated summary of everything he will say in Hebrews.

(13:1) Let brotherly love continue. Forget not love of strangers: for by it some have entertained angels unawares. Remember those in bonds, as bound with; the ill-treated as being yourselves also in body. Marriage, in honor among all, and the bed undefiled, for fornicators and adulterers the God will judge. Not fond of money, the attitude; content with what you have. For himself has said,
> I will in no way fail you,
> Neither will I in any way forsake you.

So that we boldly say,
> The Lord is my helper; I will not fear:
> What will man do to me?

Remember those ruling over you that spoke to you the word of the God. Of whom, contemplating the outcome of their behavior, imitate their faith. Jesus Christ the same yesterday and today, and unto the ages. Be not carried away by diverse and strange teachings: for it is good that the heart be established by grace; not by meats, in which they that walked were not profited.

The seminal summary he inserted was "Jesus Christ the same yesterday, and today, and unto the ages". This one statement destroys all the philosophy, propaganda, and false teachings that attempt to rear their head against the word. "Christ Jesus" is used by scripture when referring to his character as risen from the dead; "Jesus Christ" is used when referring to his character as a mortal man. So on the surface it looks like a contradiction; did not Paul say "if even we have known Christ according to flesh, yet now we know [him so] no longer"? Did not his mortal life end? Did he not say "for also the things concerning me have an end"?

It is the point he made in the book's climax of chapter ten; "a body have you prepared me". It is this living mortal human life upon which the fate of the entire universe hangs: the counseling and creating of it ("yesterday"), the preservation and continuance of it ("today"), and the fate of what will happen to it ("unto the ages"). Yes, Christ is resurrected now, and no longer mortal. But that one life, symbolized figuratively and literally by blood, is what everything rests upon, *and that never changes*.

We might note the seven teachings surrounding this point; hospitality, empathy, integrity, contentedness, courage, and respect precede it, and simplicity follows it.

The writer now is going to throw a broad principle at us—too large to have included in the body of his treatise. The experience of leaving "the camp" leads us to muse on just what "the camp" is so that we can avoid it. That is not the point at all. "The camp" is not Jewish ritual, professing Christianity, or any 'bad' thing at all. It refers to <u>every</u> organization of any kind: church, family, nationality, or any group in which we find ourselves. Sound severe? "If any man come to me, and will not hate his own father, and mother, and wife, and children, and brothers, and sisters, yes, and his own life too, he cannot be my disciple. Whoever does not carry his cross and come after me cannot be my disciple." It does not say, "prefer being a disciple above the love he has for his mother", it says "hate". Yes, Jesus said that. The writer is *hinting*—not explaining—at what it takes to follow Jesus. He is not in our church. He is not in our family. He is not in our culture. He is outside, on a cross.

(10) We have an altar, of which they have no right to eat that

serve the tabernacle. For the bodies of those beasts whose blood is brought into the holies through the high priest for sin are burned outside the camp. For this reason Jesus also, that he might sanctify the people through his own blood, suffered outside the gate. Let us therefore go forth unto him outside the camp, bearing his reproach. For we have not here an abiding city, but we seek after one to come.

There were plenty of believers in Jesus who still served the tabernacle, as Acts tells us. The writer is drawing a line in the sand and saying: 'No. You cannot do both.' Even Paul did not go this far.

He has contrasted us *not* having "here an abiding city" with that which we *do have*: an altar at which to eat. This is a spiritual altar—meaning *more* real; part of the greater reality—which we *do* use here in these present bodies, as he will say in the next two sentences.

(15) Through him therefore let us offer up sacrifice of praise to the God continually, that is, fruit of lips confessing to his name. But forget not well-doing and fellowship; for with such sacrifices the God is well pleased.

Sacrificing at an eternal altar in the previously inaccessible heavens is that easy. At least it is for those who do not resist God. Or those that watch over them, whether done well or not:

(17) Obey those ruling over you, and submit: for *they* watch in behalf of your souls, as they that will give account; that they may do this with joy, and not groaning: for this, unprofitable for you.

After all those severe words of warning, he is still open to their help and asks for prayer. And he does not say 'We are doing the work of God!' like so many, but 'we are persuaded'. 'We desire to behave honorably.' Humility is rarely used by those who feel that they must wield authority, but is part of walking the path of faith. We are all moving forward together, and one person's "riches" in spiritual knowledge does not recuse him working together with the "poor".

(18) Pray for us: for we are persuaded that we have a good conscience, desiring to behave honorably in all things. And I exhort the more exceedingly to do this, that I be restored to you the sooner.

Being restored to them is the first clue we get as to the writer's circumstances. He has consistently spoken in the plural up until now (we are persuaded better things) except for in quotes and briefly in chapter eleven (And what more may I be saying? For the time will fail me if I tell of…). It is an open question if the writer of the last three verses at the end is *someone else* appending a note regarding the writer, whom we would suppose to be Timothy. If someone unknown wrote it all, he mentions the *only* contemporary name of any person (Timothy) there for no apparent reason, *after* closing. It seems more likely that scripture is giving us a large hint that Timothy himself is the writer, and the person copying and sending the epistle (essay, really) added that note at the end. If so, it was someone who was accompanying Timothy, not vice versa; "if *he* come shortly, *I* will see you."

(20) Now the God of the peace, who brought again from dead the great shepherd of the sheep in blood of eternal covenant, our Lord Jesus, perfect you in every good work into the doing his

will, working in us what is well-pleasing in his sight through Jesus Christ; to whom the glory unto the ages of the ages. Amen.

He cannot resist throwing another secret at us before closing: that it was *part of* the Eternal Covenant to "bring back again from dead the great shepherd of the sheep". He had said "I am the good shepherd. The good shepherd lays down his life for the sheep". Romans says "Christ was raised from dead through the glory of the Father" and here this missing element is added to round it out. We are led to be curious as to how much the writer of Hebrews could have added on this subject, as well as how much more we can discover with the Spirit guiding us.

The switch to "working in us" above is a manuscript variation, but fits with him putting himself back on the same ground as his audience after so many words. Or *bits* as he says next.

(22) But I exhort you, brethren, bear with the word of the exhortation: for in bits I have written to you.

(23) Know the brother Timothy has been set free; with whom, if he come shortly, I will see you.
Greet all the ones leading you, and all the saints. They of Italy greet you. The grace *be* with you all.

End of Part IV

Takeaways:
- There is a freshly killed yet living way to enter the heavens.
- Sinning willfully disqualifies us from being part of the household of God.
- The Path of Faith has the following elements:
    - Benefit (reward) to ourselves
    - Promise of an inheritance
    - Preparation of things for us by God, that leads us to prepare for our hope
    - Discovery that the world is too limited for us
    - Accomplishing anything
    - Rejection of help or deliverance that would compromise our faith.
- We are working together with the Old Testament saints as well as many others.
- We are in a race.
- God chastens us but not those who contaminate sanctification.
- We are headed somewhere indescribable, but there are a lot of beings there including God.
- Jesus Christ the same yesterday, and today, and unto the ages.
- Outside the camp, which is any organization at all, we find Jesus.
- We can make a sacrifice suited to the eternal realm just by singing.
- Timothy probably wrote Hebrews but we do not know for sure.

Conclusion

The writer of Hebrews has lead us through the <u>rest of apostleship</u> and the <u>service of priesthood</u>. These two themes showed us man's place in the created universe, the establishment of God's house, God's rest, the approach to God, and the city of God. On Christ's part he showed us Sonship, the Sent Apostle, the house builder, the Covenant Securer, the Intercessor, the Author and Finisher of our faith, and the resurrected Shepherd. On our part he showed us adoption, companionship, present-ness (English does not have a word for being *here* and *now*), rest with God, purification, partakers of the heavenly calling, fellowship with the heavenly company, and true sacrifice.

The Content in James

James is considered a practical epistle that largely ignores doctrine. This is horsey malarkey. James is considered one of the earlier epistles. This is donkey malarkey. James is considered to be in resistance to Paul's doctrine. This is camel marlarkey and contradicts the donkey malarkey. James is considered to be all about works. This is monkey malarkey.

When we read various exegeses of James, we are struck by how much they have in common. The primary approach seems to be having a long list of what New Testament doctrine is, checking to what James mentions from the list, then concluding, "Nope, James does not deal with doctrine." Maybe toss the list and read James?

Let us go through and look at his points.

(1:1) James, of God and Lord Jesus Christ, bondman, to the twelve tribes, those in the dispersion, greeting.

The "dispersion" refers to Israelites who are not in Jerusalem, as in John 7:35 and First Peter 1:1. He is not *excluding* the gentiles, but expecting that the responsibility to be a "city situated on top of a hill" would fall first to the Jews in each city. This is apparent from the fact that he expects them to be meeting in synagogues yet it is the elders of the *assembly*, not the synagogue, that are called when one is sick. And the people *today* who are represented by the "dispersion" are quite simply the Christians who have grown up *familiar* with the elements of Christianity, just as these Jews he was writing to were already familiar with the scriptures.

His writing has reference to the writings of Paul, Peter, the gospel writers; the reader is expected to be familiar with them. He is intimately familiar with the Old Testament. He takes us up on the same ground that Hebrews twelve does: a company of people who are approaching God and have been since the beginning of mankind. This perspective takes a great deal more sophistication to express properly than a 'church age' centric view, and James handles it with refreshing expertise.

The first thing he says will be key to the rest of the epistle:

(2) Count it all joy, my brothers, when you fall into manifold temptations;

These are specifically the temptations that he spells out later (in case we have ignored his very first line); "...each is tempted, being drawn away by his own lust, and enticed. Then the lust, when it has conceived, bears sin: and the sin full grown brings forth death." *He begins his epistle by saying to rejoice when we are tempted by our own lust, then sin, and then **fall**.* That is what it says. It does not say "when you have a tough time because people are criticizing for being a jerk and you'd like to think it's because you're a Christian so you call it a trial." This is *not* someone who is going to provide 'practical ministry' to help us to be 'better Christians'. Throughout the epistle he will be saying things *that are too radical for us to read*, so we read 'around' his points and moralize them to avoid them. James is not moralizing. James is doing away with moralizing and starts off with the same points that the writer of Hebrews takes ten chapters to get to.

(3) knowing that the proving of your faith works patience.

Note that he assumes that when we fall we get right back up and keep going. The only instruction he offers in *that* regard is to "count it all joy" as we get back up. "Continuance of good works" would not take patience if there was no failure from which to learn. Christ's patience does not involve failure. Ours does. *But Christ's intercessory work sees to it that our sins are purified and we are "cleaned from all unrighteousness"*. We do not need to be cleaned if we are not dirty. Once cleaned, we are not dirty. James is taking First John 1 and combining it with Romans 2 in a way that pushes us forward in full confidence, not only *despite* our failures, but *because of* Christ's 'over-abounding' provision of grace as the result of our failures. The measure of confidence in God that is being presented here is so far beyond 'moralizing' that it doesn't even enter in. As such, he can immediately begin sketching out our path forward and the elements necessary to it. They are not 'be good' or 'don't fail', they concern patience, endurance, wisdom, spiritual vision, and a clear description of the exact kind of character it will produce in those who pursue it. *And* what will prevent it.

(4) But let patience have perfect work, that you be perfect and entire, lacking in nothing. But if any of you lacks wisdom, let him ask of the God, who gives to all simply and upbraids not; and it will be given him. But let him ask in faith, nothing doubting: for who doubts is like a sea wave, driven by wind and tossed. For let not that man think that he will receive anything of the Lord; a double-minded man, unstable in all his ways.

The word "doubleminded" is literally "two-souled", a reference to "You cannot serve God and Mammon". This produces "doubt" because our divided allegiance does not allow us to distinguish between our wants that come from our "lust" and our wants that are the result of godly boldness, as he will explain in chapter four.

This emphasis on perfect work of patience, us being "perfect", "entire", "lacking in nothing" is remarkable. He does not attribute it to holiness, obedience, sanctification of the Spirit, or any of the things which we would be tempted to insert. He attributes it to patience. He has already dismissed failure as not a danger and relegated it to a helpful role. This is what he is teaching. He wants us to be "perfect and entire, lacking in nothing", not 'avoiding failure at all costs'. The only thing he can imagine that we might lack is wisdom, and that just happens to be free at all times from a God who does not even scold us for not having it. Though having our *own* wisdom creates problems, as he is obliged to point out:

(9) But let the humble brother glory in his exaltation and the rich in his humiliation. Because as a flower of grass he will pass away; for the sun has risen with the scorching, and it has withered the grass; and its flower is fallen, and the comeliness of its face is perished; thus also will the rich fade away in his goings.

This poetic language is quite specific as to the process that those who are "rich" in scriptural knowledge go through. While *the word of God* is eternal, it is also *alive*. Static knowledge of a living entity will quickly find itself lacking. First the sun rises (a new day or a new situation) with its scorching (new difficulties), which withers the grass (the circumstances left over from the previous day), and its flower (the acclaimed carrier of doctrine from the day before) is fallen (cannot rise to meet the new difficulty), and the comeliness (suitability, literally) of its face (ability to look forward) is perished.

With this next paragraph, James returns to his theme, which is not works but endurance.

(12) Blessed *the* man that endures temptation; for when he has been approved, he will receive the crown of life, which He promised to them that love him.

Note the extreme precision with which James handles the subject of us enduring our own failures. We do not just get up and keep going, we wait for Christ's *approval*. Sin, before it is addressed, is quite distinctly sin. Further, the crown of life is not promised to those who confess their sins and get cleaned up, necessary as that might be, but the promise hinges on the only thing that will *motivate* us to keep going; we love him. This "crown of life" is the same thing that Jesus promises to those who were being tried in Revelation 2.

And lest we get the idea that we can be proud of our failures because they are somehow 'necessary' to approach God, James nails the source of our failure:

(13) Let no one say when tempted, 'I am tempted from God'; for the God is unversed in evils, and he himself tempts no one: but each is tempted, being drawn away by his own lust, and enticed. Then the lust, when it has conceived, bears sin: and the sin full grown brings forth death. Be not deceived, my beloved brothers.

In other words, 'Don't fool yourselves. Christ may be able to bring great things out of your difficulties, but you are the only one to blame for them.' God being "unversed in evils" gives the sense; it is literally 'not tempted of evil'.

Note that he likens this process to adultery. Tempted… drawn away by lust… enticed… conceiving… bearing sin… sin full grown… which imagery he alludes to again in 2:10 and 4:4. The contrast is between "sin" bringing forth "death" and the "Word of Truth" bringing forth "us". He has a clear view of what Paul means when he says "I espoused you to one husband, that I might present pure virgin to the Christ. But I fear, lest somehow, as the serpent beguiled Eve in his craftiness, your thoughts should be corrupted from the simplicity and the purity that is toward the Christ."

The "simplicity" and "purity" Paul mentions characterize our relationship with not just Christ, but God himself, who provides us perfection that goes all the way back to his eternal counsels.

(17) Every good giving and every perfect gift is from above, coming down from the Father of the lights, with whom is no variation, neither shadow cast by turning. With counsel he brought us forth by Word of Truth, that we be a kind of firstfruits of his creatures.

He is referring to Jeremiah 31, the verses immediately *after* what Hebrews twice quotes regarding a new covenant and Paul alludes to in Second Corinthians 3: "…who gives the sun for light by day, the ordinances of the moon and of the stars for light by night, who stirs up the sea so that the waves thereof roar,— Jehovah of hosts is his name: If those ordinances depart from before me, says Jehovah, the seed of Israel also shall cease from being a nation before me for ever. Thus says Jehovah: If the heavens above can be measured, and the foundations of the earth searched out beneath, I will also cast off the whole seed of Israel, for all that they have done, says Jehovah." He tells us of a God who does not change his mind one whit, who brought us forth with counsel, and delights in giving gifts to us *new* creatures—

while not changing his mind about Israel. When Paul talks about this subject he bursts into "O depth of riches and wisdom and knowledge of God! how unsearchable his judgments, and untraceable his ways!" James simply points out that given a God whose counsels do not vary, who has made us into some kind of firstfruits that we can barely understand, it might behoove us to listen more than talk.

(19) So that, my beloved brothers, let every man be swift into the hearing, slow into the speaking, slow into wrath. For man's wrath works not God's righteousness.

Odd that he would bring in wrath in this context. He is foreshadowing what he will have to get into later; false righteous indignation that has for its source jealousy and judgment. This is a pattern that is quite insidious, and James goes at it from several potent angles. When the point of a journey is to move forward, those who wish to hold back will find fault with those who put their faith on the line and venture out. This kind of judging looks holy to the onlookers, and left unchecked, can halt progress for an entire company. Hebrews in this regard says "lest any root of bitterness springing up trouble you, and many be defiled by it". Here James simply calls it "man's wrath", but later will elaborate that "this is not the wisdom that comes down from above, but earthly, sensual, demonish." For the simple soul who might be taken in by pious sounding words which overflow with wickedness, he points out that one thing it is *not*, is "meekness".

(21) For which reason putting away all filthiness and overflowing of wickedness, receive with meekness the implanted word, which *is* able to save your souls.

It might be good to note that the New Testament consistently attributes the saving of the *soul* to the continuing intercessory work of Christ, not our initial receiving of salvation. Peter elaborates on this, with the writer of Hebrews adding the requisite structure. James is not talking of being saved, he is describing the process of taking up the faith of Jesus Christ our Lord and becoming a doer of work, blessed in his doing. That is what will save the soul.

(22) But be doers of word, and not hearers only, deluding yourselves. For if any is hearer of word and not doer, this one is like a man beholding his natural face in a mirror: for he considers himself and goes away and immediately forgets what manner he was. But who looks into perfect law, that of the liberty, and abides, being not a hearer that forgets but a doer of work, this man will be blessed in his doing.

That was a masterpiece of doctrine. Paul might have gone on to explain the Law of Liberty, but James is content to simply mention it, saving it for later use in a more powerful context. Here he compares someone who hears without doing to one under Mosaic law who uses that law as a mirror to check himself then goes away and does nothing. The contrast is with one who looks into the perfect law of liberty and abides and does God's work. When we are constantly checking, forgetting, and doing nothing, our only recourse is to talk about all the good that we are doing to deceive our heart. When we abide and do, our interests are aligned with God's, which keeps us from "friendship with the world" on which he will elaborate later. Anyone reading this would be intensely curious as to just what this "perfect law, that of the liberty" is, and James does not disappoint; he will hit this subject in chapter two and drive the nails into the coffin of law-teachers in chapter four.

Meanwhile for those who are desperately looking for something to do that makes them 'good'—James calls this religious, which simply means 'ritualist'—the first thing to do is shut up about it. The second is make a ritual out of noting those who really need help, and do so without the influence of the 'world' which wants to makes a big deal about it.

(26) If any thinks to be religious, not bridling his own tongue but deceiving his own heart, the religion of this one is vain. Pure religion and undefiled before our God and Father is this, to visit orphans and widows in their affliction, keeping oneself unspotted from the world.

So now he lays out what can *prevent* the patient endurance that keeps us going even when we fall.

(2:1) My brothers, are you holding the faith of Jesus Christ our Lord of the glory with respect of persons? For if a man come into your synagogue with a gold ring in brilliant clothing and a poor man also come in mean clothing, and you have regard to him that wears the brilliant clothing, and say, Sit you here well; and you say to the poor, *you* stand or sit there under my footstool. Did you not discriminate among yourselves, and become judges with evil thoughts?

The subtle reference to "a gold ring in a swine's snout" from Proverbs eleven is classic James. He will go on several diatribes against the "rich" and the incredible amount of damage they do; here he is pointing out that the source of the problem is that we put them on a pedestal in the first place. All that damage caused by *us* wanting to be judges—which always produces evil thoughts—could have been easily prevented.

But James is saying much more here than just his example of favoritism. What does discrimination have to do with evil thoughts except in a superficial manner that we should pretend the homeless fellow who wandered in doesn't smell like a wet dog? If we remember his flower of grass example, it becomes a lot clearer. When Paul lays out church order in First Corinthians twelve through fourteen, he does not say, "Find those who have a theological degree, or know the scriptures thoroughly, and put them in charge", he says "but much rather the members of the body which seem to be weaker are necessary; and those of the body which we esteem to be more dishonored, these we invest with more abundant honour; and our indecent parts have more excessive respectability." The attitude of being judges becomes systemic, and we even apply these evil thoughts to our own bodies. In American society, we 'judged' two vital organs that the immune system depends on—the tonsils and the appendix—to be unnecessary and removed them for no reason. Then we feel good about how smart we are. This is an example of how strong the desire runs to be to be 'judges' and usurp God.

(2:5) Listen, my beloved brothers; did not the God choose the poor as to the world, rich in faith, and heirs of the kingdom which he promised to them that love him? But *you* have dishonored the poor. Do not the rich oppress you, and themselves drag you before judgment seats? Do not *they* blaspheme the honorable name by which you are called?

Most of us do not think about this. When a church splits, who builds the argument that splits it, the doctrinally rich or the untaught poor? When the decision is made to burn someone at the stake, who makes the decision; the doctrinally rich or the untaught poor? When we repeat a creed that is not in the Bible, who writes the creed; the doctrinally rich or the untaught poor?

While the poor man is not rich in scriptural knowledge, he *is* rich in faith. The kind who are heirs of the kingdom which he promised to them that love him. The kind who get back up when they fall and receive the crown of life, which he promised to them that love him. James is pounding the point home that two people sitting beside each other, one rich in scriptural knowledge and the other rich in faith, might do well to see themselves as God sees them.

Next James dives right into pure 'doctrine' in such a way that those that are looking for doctrine miss it entirely. He has already removed issues that Jesus said would prevent the word from having any effect *at all*, and he does it in order: (1) doubt in verse six, (2) confidence in possessions in verse ten, (3) blaming God for our failures in verse thirteen, (4) hearing and not doing in verse twenty-two, (5) refusal to repent in verse twenty-four, (6) doing works to be seen and bragging about them in verse twenty-six, and (7) respecter of persons at the beginning of chapter two. The seven things James has listed <u>will prevent us from having any part in the faith of Jesus in the first place</u>. Here are Jesus' words about the seven:

1. Doubt: "No one having laid his hand on plow and looking back is fit for the kingdom of God."
2. Confidence in Possessions: "But God said to him, Fool, this night will your soul required of you; and whose will be what you have prepared? Thus is he who lays up treasure for himself, and is not rich toward God."
3. Blaming God for our failures: "But the things which go forth out of the mouth come out of the heart, and those defile man. For out of the heart come forth evil thoughts, murders, adulteries, fornications, thefts, false witnessings, blasphemies".
4. Hearing and not doing: "And every one who hears these

my words and does not do them, he shall be likened to a foolish man, who built his house upon the sand; and the rain came down, and the streams came, and the winds blew and beat upon that house, and it fell, and its fall was great."

5. Refusal to repent: "And all the people who heard, and the tax-gatherers justified God, having been baptized with the baptism of John; but the Pharisees and the lawyers rendered null as to themselves the counsel of God, not having been baptized by him."
6. Doing works to be seen and bragging about them: "*You* are they who justify themselves before men, but God knows your hearts; for what among men is highly thought of is an abomination before God."
7. Respecter of persons: "How *can* you believe, who receive glory one of another, and seek not the glory, that from God alone?"

When we are doing these things, we are not 'slipping up', *we are excluding ourselves from being able to follow Jesus at all.*

Now he dovetails the last one, respecter of persons, with one of the clearest explanations of how law works found in the New Testament. This took Paul the first seven chapters of Romans to explain.

(8) However if *law* you are royally fulfilling, according to the scripture 'you will love your neighbor as yourself', you do well. But if you are being partial, you are working sin, being exposed by the law as transgressors.

The subtlety that he points out is this: the standard by which we compare ourselves to each other (respecter of persons) is how good we look to each other. The standard for looking good is law, and the highest law regarding each other is 'You will love your neighbor as yourself'. When we love our neighbor as ourself except for the ones that do not look good (partiality) we have just broken the very law that we use for looking good in the first place. James is an expert at turning things on their head like this. *And* he is making the same exact point that Paul spends the second half of Romans chapter two explaining.

He then uses *this* principle to point out the futility of using law as a standard in the first place:

(10) For whoever will keep the whole law, and offend in one, is become guilty of all. For who said, Do not commit adultery, said also, Do not kill. Now if you do not commit adultery, but kill, you are become transgressor of law.

Those who think that he was somehow propping up law need to read this a few times. With James it is all or nothing, and while Paul will spend many chapters putting law in its proper perspective, James goes straight to the bottom line: judgment. The judgment of the law on us is condemnation if we break one commandment. Since we *are* to be judged, and Moses' law condemns us, what is it that we will be judged by? A different law, that of liberty.

(12) So speak, and so do, as those to be judged by Law of Liberty. For the judgment without mercy to him that has shown no mercy: mercy glories against judgment.

And that is all he has to say on the subject. What he has done is take Jesus' words about judgment "Judge not, that you may not be judged; for with what judgment you judge you will be judged; and with what measure you measure, it will be measured to you" and applied his words regarding the "weightier matters of the law: judgment and mercy and faith" to show that *the Mosaic law itself* was preparation for the new Law of Liberty because it prepared people to be treated according to their actions. Only one of the ten commandments has a consequence attached, *and it is a positive one* (that it may be well with you, and that you may be long lived on the earth, as Paul quotes it.) But without consequence law is of no effect. And he has already pointed out that breaking any one law has the same result of breaking all of them: condemnation. In Acts he agreed with Peter's words, "Why do you tempt God by putting a yoke upon the neck of the disciples which neither our fathers nor we have been able to bear?" So his respect for what Moses delivered allows him to see that there was no disagreement between *the object* of Mosaic law (judgment, mercy, and faith) and the law of liberty.

In other words, James clearly sees an unbroken transition from the old law of commandments to the new law of Christ. So he can say "mercy glories over judgment" which statement holds true regardless of being "under law" (as Paul puts it) or not. He introduces the law of the Christ with a new and unique term: the Law of Liberty. He understood "if therefore the Son will set you free, you will be really free." But the law of liberty has immediate consequence; not based on an injunction that must be followed, but on the question of how we use this new freedom. James is pointing out that just as we are free from doing the commandments of the law, we are also free to perform the intentions of the law. Paul puts this "in order that the righteous requirement of the law be fulfilled in us, who do not walk according to flesh but according to Spirit" and leaves out the aspect of judgment. James includes it, and tells us what it will be like. We will be judged according to how we use our freedom.

Having knocked over the idol they were making of freedom, he moves on to the idol they were making out of faith.

(14) What the benefit my brothers, if one say he has faith, but have not works? Can the faith save him? If a brother or sister be naked, and lacking daily food and one of you say to them, 'Go in peace! Be warmed! And be satisfied!' and you are not giving them the bodily needs; what the benefit? Even so the faith, if it have not works, is dead in itself.

This is not merely *proving* faith by works, as we will see by his examples, but the *completion* of faith. And he is certainly not arguing with Paul who said to the Thessalonians, "remembering unceasingly your work of faith". Paul contrasted faith with works *of law*, but those who twist Paul's words would contrast faith with *any works at all* as if saying that merely believing something can save us. James is pointing out that if "faith is the *substantiating* of things hoped for" that there needs to be something substantial to be substantiated. Peter has a good line on the subject "the proving of your faith, much more precious than of gold which perishes"; he speaks of "receiving the end of your faith, salvation of souls" and "in your faith have virtue". But only James gives us the nitty-gritty of the *process* of finishing—that is, perfecting—faith. First he gives an example to illustrate the complexity of the issue:

(18) But any can say, 'You are having faith, and I am having works? Show me your faith apart from the works, and I by my works will show you the faith...

The point is not complicated, but he is talking to people who complicate it. Faith and works cannot be distinguished in our day-to-day actions without making judgments, which leads to interminable arguments and evil thoughts. Once again, James hits the bottom line as he continues his example of a dialogue:

(19) '...*You* believe that God is one? you do well: the demons also believe, and shudder. But will you know, O vain man, that the faith apart from the works is dead? . . .

In other words, all the faith in the world does not differentiate us from a demon if we do not think that any works need accompany it.

But James kindly spells it out for us as he continues his dialogue:

(21) '...Was not Abraham our father justified by works, in that he offered up Isaac his son upon the altar? You see that the faith wrought with the works, and by the works was the faith perfected; and the scripture was fulfilled which says, And he—Abraham—believed God, and it was reckoned to him for righteousness; and he was called God's friend.'

The example he uses shows his remarkable grasp of scripture. The scripture that is being fulfilled was the promise to Abraham when he was 85 (Genesis 15:6) when the 430 years began; Paul says that the covenant was confirmed then and Exodus tells us that they came out of Egypt on their completion. The *fulfillment* of this scripture—when he offered up Isaac—was thirty years later when the *400 years* began, prophesied to Abraham in 15:15 and reiterated by Stephen in Acts 7:6. Abraham was 115 years old and Isaac was 15 when he perfected—finished—the faith which was reckoned to him as righteousness when he was 85. Hebrews six refers to this finishing—quoting Genesis 22—as Abraham getting the promise after long patience. Exactly one thousand years later Jehoshaphat was in the eighth year of his reign; the same Jehoshaphat who used the phrase "Abraham your friend" which James quotes here; Hebrews calls this the *witness* of faith and uses Abel and Enoch as examples. In fact Hebrews eleven takes what James has laid out here and details the seven stages of *perfecting* our faith into an entire chapter, with examples (including, again, Rahab).

- **Witness** to God by us, and by God of us (1-5)
- **Promise** and inheritance from God and preparation and action by us (7-13)
- **Desire** for God by us and preparation by God of an inheritance (14-22)
- **Rejection** of the limitations of this world by us and deliverance from God (23-31)
- **Accomplishments** by participation with God (32-35)
- **Not accepting deliverance** from the world (36-38)
- **Receiving** the promise and inheritance by return of the initial **witness** by God (39)

James is pointing out that God reckoning Abraham's faith at 85 as righteousness was perfected when Abraham was 115 by the act of offering up his son. The implications dovetail with Peter's laying out of the subject: that the proving of your faith, much more precious than of gold which perishes, though it is proved by fire, be found to praise and glory and honour at revelation of Jesus Christ whom, having not seen, you love; on whom, though now you see him not, but believing, you rejoice greatly with joy unspeakable and filled with glory; receiving the end of your faith, salvation of souls. Concerning which salvation prophets sought and searched diligently, who prophesied of the grace that is unto you; searching what, or what manner of time, the Spirit of Christ which was in them did point unto, when he testified beforehand the sufferings unto Christ, and the glories after them. To whom it was revealed, that not to *themselves* but to *you* did they minister these things which have now been announced to you by those who have declared to you the glad tidings by Holy Spirit sent from heaven, which angels desire to look into. Peter is saying that the proving of our faith ends in salvation of souls, related to what he says later about "purifying your souls". It is in this context that the *process* of *perfecting* faith occurs; indeed, the ministry of many Old Testament writers was not even "to themselves". The rest of his quote is relevant in this context as it connects Hebrews' treatment of faith with James', and lest we think this is a simple subject, he mentions that angels desire to look into it; showing how God has us working on issues shared by beings from other ages and seasons.

So James insisting on works accompanying faith is not a nice comment that 'we should do things, not just believe', but an overview of how faith works—*and has always worked*—in mortals. It is believed by the heart then proved with action. Both are necessary, as Paul says in Romans 10:10 regarding salvation.

James ends the "But any can say..." dialogue with this point (the "you" in the next verse reverts back to the plural used in the rest of the epistle to address his readers) and summarizes for us. And of course he has to hit us up with another example:

(24) You see that by works a man is justified, and not by faith alone. And likewise was not also Rahab the harlot justified by works, in that she received the messengers, and to a different way sent?

Again, the faith was *expressed* and the promise *secured* by Rahab first, but it was her act of letting them down by a cord through the wall that was the means of identifying the house of safety when Israel destroyed the city. It was her act of sending them to the mountains for three days that protected them from the pursuers. She did these things after *already having received their promise*. This was not the *having* of faith, this was the *proving* of faith. And it is evident that God honored the proving with his own proof; her house was on the same wall that fell flat when the priests blasted on the trumpets and the people shouted, and was preserved. And lest we think that the 400 year / 430 year question which James so neatly wraps up happened by chance, notice the timing of the one example James picked out of the entire Old Testament; Rahab would have married Salmon, David's great-great-grandfather, exactly 430 years after Isaac married Rebecca.

Note that without the 400/430 year question being solved, we do not have an unbroken chronology of scripture. We have Adam to Abraham, and we have Moses to Jesus, but Abraham to Moses depends on the understanding of this single point which James solves for us. Without taking James seriously we have no scripture chronology.

And he is not content to leave it at that; he has to emphasize which of the two, faith or works, is the lasting element in the duality. Hebrews six, when speaking to people who are clearly avoiding the exercise of faith, expresses it like this: "the God is not unrighteous to forget your *work* and the love which you showed toward his name, in that you ministered unto the saints, and do minister. And we desire that each of you show the same diligence unto the fullness of the hope even to the end: that you be not sluggish, but imitators of them who through *faith* and patience inherit the promises."

Paul points out that grace is the source of salvation and real faith is the means of salvation. James points out that we can think we have real faith but only God can judge; we are very good at fooling ourselves. Someone who does the work of God but does not realize that he has faith can still be identified by the fact that he is bearing fruit. These are called "the meek" by Jesus, who said, "by their *fruits* you will know them." Thus, for us, the danger is not that the *works* are dead because they might not really have faith behind them: the danger is that the *faith* is dead because it has no works at all behind it.

(26) Just as the body apart from spirit is dead, even so the faith apart from works is dead.

Having established how we are to be judged and how we are to perfect our faith, he moves on to the pivot of his letter. The *climax* will come later when he tells us how to draw near to God. Here we get the *pivot*, which is the one thing we physically do that always has spiritual ramifications: yap.

(3:1) Be not many teachers, my brothers, knowing that we will receive greater condemnation, for we all offend much. If any offend not in word, this is a mature man, able to bridle the whole body also.

James expects us to be familiar with the difference between speaking evil and doing evil. The spiritually intelligent of Old or New Testament saints could easily point out how speaking evil can lead to far worse things than merely doing it; or how one can get "trapped" and "seized with the words of your mouth" as Proverbs puts it. So what is James bringing here that is new? One, that "teaching" *necessarily* offends, exacerbating any offense already occurring. Note that if people are hanging around looking for excuses to get offended, sometimes it is perfectly proper to do so; Jesus did this frequently.

But James switches from offending others to bridling our own body with a dizzying series of analogies. First point is that being able to control the mouth is like bridling the whole body. When he switches to horses, it's *us* bridling *their* mouth to turn around *their* body. When he switches to ships, it's the steersman controlling the rudder which then controls the ship in the face of rough winds attempting to usurp this control.

(3) Now if we put the bits of horses into the mouths that they may obey us, we turn about their whole body also.

James quoting Psalm 32 to round out Paul's quote of it in Romans 4:7 regarding works; "Even as David also declares the blessedness of the man to whom God reckons righteousness apart from works:
>Blessed, whose iniquities are forgiven,
>And whose sins are covered.
>Blessed, man to whom the Lord will not reckon sin."

Ironically, this psalm discusses how David did not want to confess his transgression, but finally did. The entire psalm is an instruction of how to interact with God's directing, and James is highly suggesting that we read it. Verses 8 and 9 say "I contemplate you, and direct you this way, the way you go; on you my eye counsels. Be you not as horse, as mule without understanding; adorned with restraining bit and bridle or they do not approach you." In other words, 'If we are not mature enough to bit our tongue and bridle our body, God will have to do it for us.' He points out that the pressures of having "bitter jealousy and faction in your heart" are from resisting the confession of our sins to God: "When I kept silent, my bones disintegrated in me in my roaring all day long" in verse 3. He now addresses this idea of turning about "their whole body":

(4) Lo, the ships also, though they are so great and are driven by rough winds, are turned about by a very small rudder, to where the impulse of the steersman wills. Thus the tongue also is a little member, and boasts greatly.

The subject here is just who is in control of the turning which is the subject of Isaiah 30 and worth reading in this context. In verse 21 it says "And your ears, they hear a word from behind you saying, 'This is the way, walk in it' when you turn to the right or to the left." He is dealing with the intricate subject of *who controls the controls*? It is the rudder that turns the ship around, but the helmsman who steers it, as Paul says "So then it is not of him that wills, nor of him that runs, but of God that shows mercy." But this control can be usurped at any point in the process by someone in the line of command thinking that he is in charge. God often waits for us to play out our fantasy of having control; verse 18 says, "therefore will Jehovah wait, that he may be gracious to you." The scripture James will allude to next regarding our tongue being a fire is verse 27, not about *our* tongue being a fire, but *Jehovah's*: "Behold, the name of Jehovah comes from far, his anger burning—heavy with issues; his lips are full of indignation, and his tongue as a consuming fire, and his breath as an overflowing torrent, which reaches even to the neck, to sift the nations with the sieve of destruction, and a bridle into the jaws of the people that cause them to go astray." However, when *we* usurp control, the fire burns out of control.

)5) Lo, how much wood is kindled by how small a fire! And the tongue—fire!

James' writing is so concentrated that it is easy to miss the depth which is always there and always intentional. He has started by contrasting us with Proverbs 26:20 "Where no wood is, the fire goes out; and where there is no talebearer, the contention ceases. Coals for embers, and wood for fire, and quarrelsome man to inflame contention." He will bring this around again to gossip in 4:11 with its effect on others and the spiritual implications; here he emphasizes the effect on *ourselves*.

(6) The tongue is 'the world of the injustice' among our members, which defiles the whole body, and sets on fire the cycle of nature, and is set on fire by hell.

This "the world of the injustice" is the evil we face every day by living in "the world". system which operates by the lust of the eyes, the lust of the flesh, and the pride of life rather than eyes focused ahead, a mortal body toward life, and the dignity of fellowship with God. It is all the evil *outside* of us that we struggle through. The tongue, however, replicates this same system *inside* us. We cannot face both at once. When a person *speaks* the whole body works together to make that speech real. When we speak *evil*, the whole body which God created to work together with integrity tries to make that evil speech real and true. The whole body becomes defiled. Lust and pride, when dignified by being verbalized in joking, criticism, or outright claims, root themselves *inside*, settling into the heart. James is giving us the actual mechanics of what Jesus said: "but the things which go forth out of the mouth come out of the heart, and those defile man." The very "cycle" or 'wheel' of nature is consumed by the fire of self-condemnation and self-judgment from which there is no escape, driving all our natural bodily actions toward self-destruction and death. James is giving us the underlying mechanics of the process Paul describes in Romans seven.

This also explains the strange saying of Jesus, "for by your words you will be justified, and by your words you will be condemned." What about our actions? Our *words* have the ability to set our hearts on one path or another. Jesus said this after saying "whoever will speak against the Holy Spirit it will not be forgiven him, neither in this age nor in the coming." This scares people because it sounds like there is a new category of sin that is 'unforgivable'. It is unforgivable, not because it is a different category, but because all our bodily actions align with our words. The fact that today words have become so cheap that no one can fathom their potential significance does not change the reality that James states here. He is quite familiar with Jesus' words in the last half of Matthew five.

And the tongue is not something that can be gently coaxed into goodness through manners and teaching it to say nice things. Either we say something or we do not. There is no 'taming' the tongue.

(7) For every kind of beasts and birds, of things creeping, and in the sea, is tamed, and has been tamed by human nature: but the tongue can no man tame: a restless evil, full of deadly poison.

The reference is to Psalm 58: "Their poison is like the poison of a serpent: like the deaf adder which stops her ear, which hears not the voice of enchanters, of one charming ever so wisely."

It is difficult to resist the rather plain example he gives next of how we are subjecting ourselves to this condemnation. Recall that he started this subject with "Be not many teachers". He is now reminding us of "by their fruits you will know them" and asking us to apply it to ourselves. Instead of telling us that it is 'wrong' to curse men, he points out that they "are made after

God's likeness". What he is pointing out is that we 'dismiss' men because they do not live up to the standard of "the Lord and Father" whom we bless; such dismissal is not something that either the angels or we have a right to do because it involves *judging* men; which he will address in 4:12. The immediate problem is the lack of integrity we show by venting different elements from the same source. There is a place for olives, and there is a place for figs; but not from the same plant.

(9) With it bless we the Lord and Father; and with it curse we the men, who are made after God's likeness. Out of the same mouth comes forth blessing and cursing. My brothers, these ought not to be thus. Does the fountain send forth from the same opening the sweet and the bitter? Can a fig tree, my brothers, yield olives, or a vine figs? Thus no spring makes salty and sweet water.

Note the care with which he presents examples. We might be tempted to take his point as 'Don't be bad and curse!' But figs are good and olives are good. He is making a case for having integrity. If we think about it, he has *consistently* been making a case for integrity; not only our own, but God's. With endurance, faith, freedom, law, works, and his other subjects, he has been knocking over our idols. These idols have primarily been the *false consistency* we impose on God's ways in order to find a way to understand them. God is consistent. We are not. Our way of finding consistency in God is to limit what he is doing to what we can understand. Fortunately we have James to wake us up to reality.

This manner in which he has led us toward the idea of integrity is a doctrinal *tour de force*. Someone who is stuck in Old Testament ideas, when talking about what part of us to put reins on, would not focus on the tongue, but the heart. Jeremiah seventeen says "The heart is deceitful above all things, and incurable; who can know it? I Jehovah search the heart, I try the reins, even to give each one according to his ways, according to the fruit of his doings." This is literally 'kidneys', not 'reins', but the point is that the Old Testament teachings regarding the *heart* outnumber the *tongue* ten to one. Yet James understands that being in Christ involves the death of the *husband* part of us (the "old man" who is subject to law as Romans 7:1-3 explains), so that the *wife* part of us (the heart) is free to be to another who is raised from the dead. In other words, one of the new elements of Christianity introduced by us having "died with Christ" as Colossians three and Romans six point out, is that the heart *can* be directed into the love of God as Second Thessalonians says, and that our hearts *can* be pure, as First Peter says. The heart is no longer a problem. The tongue is. James knows this intimately.

(13) Who is wise and understanding among you? let him show by his good conduct his works in meekness of wisdom.

We can almost hear the words of Ecclesiastes ringing in James ears as he wrote that; "Who is as the wise? and who knows the explanation of things? A man's wisdom makes his face to shine, and the boldness of his face is changed."

(14) But if you have bitter jealousy and faction in your heart, glory not and lie not against the truth. This is not the wisdom that comes down from above, but earthly, sensual, demonish. For where jealousy and faction, there: confusion and every vile deed.

James just hit the root again. It is not that jealousy and faction lead us to do things that are against the truth, it is that *we are against the truth in the first place*. The jealously and faction are in our heart. We *express* it against our brothers, but that is only the expression. What we are bitterly jealous of is how God gets to do what he wants. We do not mind when he wants to bless us, but *other people who don't deserve it?* We get upset when God gives us our denarius for working all day in the hot sun, then give the same denarius to someone who came in at the last minute and hardly did anything. "Is your eye evil because *I* am good?" Yes, our eye is evil. We look at things with the wisdom that compares, not the wisdom that is pure. Yes, our eye is evil, but that is not the problem, that is the symptom. The problem is that we have allowed faction to settle in our hearts. Some truths are 'higher' than other truths. The perfected saints are 'better' than the struggling ones. We compare ourselves to ourselves, doctrines to doctrines, beliefs to beliefs… all in an effort to own the best 'faction'. It takes a great deal of wisdom to figure out what is 'better'; the trouble is that this wisdom is earthly, sensual, and demonish.

(17) But the wisdom from above is first pure, then peaceable, gentle, easily entreated, full of mercy and good fruits, without variance, without hypocrisy.

That statement is like a drink of fresh water. There is no effort to be expended, just easily accessible goodness. No fault on our part for lacking wisdom; it is full of mercy and good fruits. And James cannot resist giving his own discovery of what these good fruits involve:

(18) And the fruit of righteousness in peace is sown to them that make peace.

He is taking Proverbs 11:30, "The fruit of righteousness is Tree of Life" and applying it to peace. He is familiar with Amos 6, "you have turned judgment into gall and the fruit of righteousness into wormwood, you that rejoice in a thing of nothing, that say, Have we not taken to us power by our own strength?" and will deal with it in 4:16. Paul had referred to being complete in this "fruit of righteousness", connecting it with being "pure and without offense". This peace is not the fruit that is *sown*, it is the necessary condition for the fruit to *grow*. The tree of life, absent since Genesis and mentioned again only in Proverbs and Revelation, is being planted to produce fruit for those who are, as Jesus said, to be called the sons of God: the peace-makers. Hebrews says the fruit of righteousness is produced when we accept the chastening of the Father, which is what can remove the "faction" that has settled in our heart that causes us to ignore books like James; "And if any one take from the words of the book of this prophecy, God shall take away his part from the tree of life", this being written in the third to last verse in the entire Bible. We can see from its placement the vehemence with which James speaks, and the appreciation God has for those who make peace, *because they are providing the ground in which is planted the tree of life*.

(4:1) From where wars and from where fightings among you? come they not from here, of your pleasures that war in your members?

As usual, James is making several powerful points simultaneously. Does he blame "wars and fightings" on "factions"? No, he has covered that point by showing us that it is the "truth" that we are lying against and glorying against, not each other. Our infighting is caused, far more banally, by *lust* and *jealousy*.

Suppose that we are in a group of Christians and get attacked by someone saying that what we are teaching is not scriptural. This happens in churches about—rough estimate—tens of thousands of times per day; in many sermons it composes the entirety of the message. What is our reaction? Do we rest in the fact that "we can do nothing against the truth, but for the truth" and see the problem for the simple jealousy that it is? Or do we attempt to defend that which needs no defense? We can *practice* the truth, *love* the truth, *know* the truth, *speak* the truth, *witness to* the truth, *rejoice with* the truth, *hear* the truth, *believe* the truth, *acknowledge* the truth, *obey* the truth, and even *gird our loins* with truth. But nowhere in all of this is there any instruction to *defend* the truth. The truth needs no defense.

When we are tempted to defend the truth what we are actually doing is responding to jealousy *with* jealousy and showing that we have the same "pleasures which war in your members" operating in *us* as in our attackers. It does not matter who has the 'right' position. What matters is who can "show by his good conduct his works in meekness of wisdom." God does not give out gold stars for being right; he is a rewarder of those who practice faith.

James will use this point to get to the climax of his epistle. In it he delivers the full range of what is possible to those in Christ. Taking up from the "pleasures which war in your members", he is again going to switch what is happening externally with what is happening internally. Paul says that it is the law of sin in our members that wars against the law of our mind; James gives the reason. Adultery. He alluded to it in 1:13 when he talked about lust, and purposefully used as examples committing adultery and killing when he brought up keeping the law in 2:10.

(2) You lust, and have not:

This is how it begins. *Every* perfect gift is from above, coming down from the Father of the lights. What on earth or in heaven could we want more? It is not *what* we want, it is *that* we want. And more importantly, it is not that we actually desire; we have forgotten how to desire. The energy we could have put into good desire is wasted on lust. When we lust, it does not matter whether we have every possible thing anyone could ever want or not. Lust, when entertained, never stops. Lust is not looking for something to *use*, it is looking for something to *use up*. If lust cannot have something, it insists that no one else have it either. In fact, given full reign, lust insists that no one else have anything at all. His point? Lust is not desire. This is the 'double mindedness' from 1:4; here it is more than divided allegiance that does not allow us to distinguish between our wants that come from our "lust" and our desires that are the result of godly boldness. It is being 'impure' (verse 8) through an adulterous relationship: marrying our "lust" (feminine) with the "the world" (masculine) to conceive "sin". James is giving yet more of the background process of Romans seven.

)2) you kill, and are jealous and obtain not:

Again, while this jealousy *expressed* toward our brothers, it is actually glorying "against the truth". It is God that we are angry at. Why did Cain get upset at Abel for offering a more excellent sacrifice? Because he was angry at God for looking at Abel's sacrifice and not his. John says he killed his brother because his works were wicked. God says his tongue is fire, but when we think we can be God and make our tongue fire and it does not have a good effect. Exodus 34 says Jehovah's name is Jealous… when we think we can be God and be jealous it works about as well as operating our tongues as fire. We think we are like God and have the right to kill. With Abel out of the way, Cain thought he could "obtain" his position in the bloodline of promise. He obtained not. Eve said when Seth was born, "He sets for me—God—seed; another after Abel; that he killed him—Cain."

Murder is the sin that is conceived by our lusting after grace given by God to someone other than ourselves. When this kind of behavior is encouraged, as it is in Christianity today, it results in a state of constant chaotic war. Note God's response to our lusting after the grace given to someone else: he gives them more. In verse six it will say "But he gives greater grace". This then upsets us even more. But God "resists the proud, but gives grace to the humble." The method we use for murder is speaking against each other, which he will explain in verse eleven. The method for speaking against each other is accusation, which is use of law and judging: "the letter kills, but the spirit gives life."

)2) you fight and war; you have not because you ask not.

In this whole process, all we have to do is ask God. The trouble is, we have no idea what we want because we have discarded desire for lust. Lust is unable to desire because true desire wants to *use* things for God, for each other, and for life. Lust wants to *use up* things for *ourselves*. Lust consumes and spends. Desire builds and enriches. The ability to desire requires maturity which comes by patience.

(3) You ask, and receive not, because you ask amiss, that you may spend in your pleasures. Adulteresses, know you not that the friendship of the world is enmity with the God? Whoever therefore intends to be the world's friend makes himself God's enemy.

James has pointed out that (1) the ground from which the tree of life is growing is being prepared by those who make peace, (2) we don't have peace, we have wars and fighting, (3) the wars *outside* come from the pleasures warring *inside* us because (4) we are not mature enough to know what to desire, and in our embarrassment we use lust instead, (5) leaving us with nothing, (6) making us jealous of those to whom God gives grace, (7) causing us to kill them, primarily by speaking against them, (8) preventing us from having the slightest idea of what to ask God, (9) causing us to ask for the only things we know how to want: pleasures to consume, (10) preventing us from receiving anything at all.

(5) Or think you that the scripture says in vain, Does the Spirit which he made to dwell in us long unto envying? But he gives greater grace.

He is referring to Numbers 11:29 where Moses points out to Joshua that there is no need for jealousy where God's Spirit is working. This little recognized fact is one of the characteristics of the Spirit which frustrates our need for control. We not only have no control over the Spirit, we can not even tell what he is going to do. This issue was quite a big deal in Acts where every effort failed by friend or foe alike to define, buy, limit, prescribe, or fool the Spirit, who quite decidedly does whatever he wants. And *God's* solution to all this is to give greater grace, primarily to the humble.

)6) For which reason it says, the God resists the proud, but gives grace to humble. Be subject therefore to the God.

The section in Proverbs from which this quote is taken (3:34) starts in verse eleven with the verses that Hebrews quotes: "My son, regard not lightly the Lord's chastening, nor faint when reproved of him; for whom the Lord loves he chastens, and scourges every son whom he receives." after which Hebrews goes on "looking carefully lest any be falling short of the grace of the God; lest any root of bitterness springing up trouble, and through this the many be defiled; lest any fornicator, or profane, as Esau". James combines these three things and calls it what it is: having an affair with the world system that we have accepted in our heart. If there is a contrast to be had, it is between welcoming the enticements of lust or withstanding the ruler of the world who uses the elements of his world to seduce our weak or inexperienced hearts.

We welcome the enticements of the flesh by falsely thinking that we desire things which we do not actually desire. We convince ourselves that we are attracted to things which we are not actually attracted to. We usually verbalize this process in pious sounding words of self depreciation. Once verbalized, our *bodies* attempt to like something that is not toward life. The *war* that is in our members is between the pleasures that are anti-life like adultery, which we give lip-service to, and the deeper understanding placed in us by our Creator that "the body apart from spirit is dead" and working together with spirit toward life. Temptation, when falsely verbalized as a reality (when in fact it is good old fashioned laziness) *becomes* a reality in us and creates wars where there need be none. The solution is not to berate our body; it is what it is. The solution is to take charge and call a spade a spade: quite simply, there is nothing that either the world or the 'pleasures' *we falsely impute* to it have to offer us. We make up pleasure where there is none, then try to convince ourselves that it is pleasurable when it is not. The solution is to face the 'world' of fake pleasure and withstand it, then face reality and approach it.

)7) Withstand the devil, and he will flee from you. Draw near to the God, and he will draw near to you.

And James has just covered the subject of desire by pointing out that all we have to do is be willing to accept reward from the only source who can give reward: God. "Who comes to the God must believe that he is, and is rewarder of them that seek after him." This is so simple to the humble as to hardly be worth the trouble of stating. To those of us who are *not* humble, however, he must elaborate.

)8) Clean your hands, sinners, and purify your hearts, double-minded. Be afflicted, and mourn, and weep: let your laughter be turned to mourning, and the joy to heaviness.

This cleanness of the hands is mentioned twice in Psalm 18 after which David says "With the gracious you show yourself gracious; with the upright man you show yourself upright; with the pure you show yourself pure; and with the perverse you show yourself cunning", something that sounds just like James. He is referencing Psalm 24:4 "he that has blameless hands and a pure heart; who lifts not up his soul unto vanity, nor swears deceitfully, he will receive blessing from Jehovah, and righteousness from the God of his salvation." Washing of the hands is conspicuously absent from the rest of the New Testament except for Pilate and the Pharisees, and here "sinners", making us wonder if James is forcing his readers into this class of people to generate repulsion.

This is also the third time he has mentioned "double-minded"; it is becoming somewhat of a theme, characterized by not getting anything; "let not that man think that he will receive anything of the Lord" until he purifies his heart.

This process of purifying the heart requires the honest evaluation of things after which we lust. "Be wretched, and mourn, and weep" is the loss and reevaluation of what we falsely held to be useful or uplifting. For example, many people would be wretched and mourn and weep if their telly, which does nothing but make them miserable while telling them that it is doing the opposite, were taken from their home. We are quite good at fooling ourselves, or being willing fools. His allusion to "as the crackling of thorns under a pot, so is the laughter of the fool" is not missed with "let your laughter be turned to mourning, and the joy to dejection."

(10) Humble yourselves in the Lord's sight and he will exalt you.

As James winds down (if it can be called that) he finishes off the points he has made by combining the ramifications. He has talked to us about law. He has talked to us about discrimination, jealousy, fighting, and factions. He has talked to us about judging. Now he combines them.

(11) Speak not one against another, brothers. Who speaks against a brother, or judges his brother, speaks against law, and judges law: but if you judge law, you are not doer of law, but judge. One is lawgiver and judge, he who can save and destroy: but who are *you* that judge the neighbor?

This point is incredibly simple, incredibly important, and incredibly ignored. To criticize is to judge. To judge is to judge law. To judge law is to usurp God. Period. Just as he has been consistently pointing out, judging our neighbor is merely a *symptom* of what is really happening: we are trying to judge

God. The one who can save or destroy us.

Now he picks up on lying against the truth, which comes from 'worldly' intentions. This simply means that our intention is to use earthly wisdom to advantage ourselves.

(13) Come now, you that say, Today or tomorrow we will go into this city, and spend a year there, and trade, and gain: since you know not what is your life on the morrow, for you are a vapor that appears for a little, and then disappears. Instead of your saying, If the Lord will, we will both live, and do this or that. But now you glory in your vauntings: all such glorying is evil.

We cannot advantage something that is too insubstantial (a "vapor") to be advantaged. Thinking that we can advantage ourselves is quite simply evil. And he makes the much needed connection between the *thought in our heart* that we can advantage ourselves instead of waiting for God to advantage us, and our *use of this attitude* to avoid doing good. For example, *today* our brother needs a cucumber, but we think that *next week* the rent is due and we might not have enough money to pay for it. Earthly wisdom says we cannot afford to get him a cucumber. Wisdom from above says ask God about it and "know" whether it is a good thing to do or not.

And in explaining this point, he gives one of only three definitions of sin in the whole New Testament.

(17) To him therefore that knows to do good, and does not, to him it is sin.

A book could be written on that subject. Not here. He now picks up on what he started in 2:9 about the "rich", which applies to anyone with knowledge of scripture. This time he waxes prophetic as well as poetic. It is the "rich" who kills the righteous, and thus kills the Righteous One. To slight a laborer in the field is to slight Christ. He starts with what Jesus says "Treasure not up for yourselves treasures upon earth, where moth consumes and rust, and where thieves dig through and steal. But treasure up for yourselves treasures in heaven, where neither moth nor rust consumes, and where thieves do not dig through nor steal: for where your treasure is, there will your heart be also." Jesus refers to "treasures on earth", and James says "You have lived delicately on the earth". We can draw from this that the "riches" of scriptural knowledge that we gather are primarily being used by us *on earth*, and has the effect of killing the righteous. Jesus reiterates this point in Revelation when he says "Because you say 'I am rich, and have become rich, and have need of nothing, and know not that you are the wretched and miserable and poor and blind and naked: I counsel you to buy of me gold refined by fire, that you be rich." There are several oddities regarding these examples, not the least of which are that real gold does not rust, and if we are to buy gold, what do we buy it with? James connects Jesus' words to Ezekiel 24:9-14 and rounds out the parable:

(5:1) Come now, the rich, weep; howl for your miseries that are coming on. Your riches are corrupted, and your garments are moth-eaten. your gold and your silver is rusted; and their rust will be for a testimony against you, and will eat your flesh as fire.

In Ezekiel the rust is incurable even though everything *in* the pot is burned up and the pot itself is heated to consume the rust on it: "yet her great rust goes not out of her: let her rust be in the fire".

The point he makes in his last diatribe against those who oppress is that *all increase that advantages us on the earth—such as learning doctrine—is done on the backs of the "poor"*, to whom Jesus said in Luke, "*yours* is the kingdom of God." James wants this to sink in. Thinking that godliness is gain, as Paul says, is a mark of "men corrupted in the mind and bereft of the truth". James finishes off his prophecy by telling us *exactly* what we are doing when we attempt to *increase* rather than *grow*.

You have laid up treasure in last days. Lo, the hire of the laborers who reap your fields, which is of you kept back, cries out: and the cries of them that reaped have entered into the ears of Lord of Sabaoth. You have lived delicately on the earth and taken pleasure; you have nourished your hearts in a day of slaughter. You condemn—you kill—the righteous; he is not resisting you.

First we oppress the easily oppressed. We have fields of knowledge in scripture and want to reap respect. So we teach people and they go through a great deal of effort to listen carefully and learn from us. Do we return that respect in kind? Do we pay those reaping our fields, and bringing us sheaves of respect and honor, by respecting and honoring their faith? "Did not the God choose the poor as to the world, rich in faith?" No. We hog the respect, take credit for *their* faith, and Jehovah of Hosts ("Lord of Sabaoth") hears their cries.

Secondly we use this respect to skip lightly over the struggles and uncertainty of the poor and wallow in confidence, unmindful of how much like Nabal we have become.

Thirdly, we replace the righteousness of God with *our* approval. When a simple believer is being chastised by God to produce the peaceable fruit of righteousness, *we* declare that he must have done something wrong; destroying both his confidence and the work of God. Our ready condemnations and pious sounding reproaches lift us up into the position of judge and shove him down into the position of slaving for our approval. But there is only one Judge who can save and destroy. Note that he did *not* address that section to "brothers".

Having dispensed with the riff-raff, so to speak, he once again addresses those whom he started with.

(7) Be patient therefore, brothers, until the presence of the Lord. Lo, the husbandman waits for the precious fruit of the earth, being patient over it, until it receive the early and latter rain. Be *you* also patient; establish your hearts because the presence of the Lord is at hand.

There is a special subject introduced here, beyond even the joy of patience of watching the plants drinking up the last goodness of the latter rain. It is *the presence of the Lord*. We are in temporary bodies operating in temporary circumstances. This does not mean that everything we are doing is going to pass away, as many teach, but that everything we are working on will be *finished* when Jesus says it is finished… which he will do *personally* to us, in rather specific and in many cases, public, ways. The presence of the Lord will "set in order" what we have struggled with for so long.

Having thoroughly dismissed judging as pure evil, he can address our tendency to get irritated with each other in a much gentler manner:

(9) Murmur not, brothers, against one another, that you be not judged: lo, the judge stands before the doors.

He is referring to Jesus' summary of what is to come in Matthew 24 and Mark 13, where he also uses "doors" plural. The reference to Psalm 24 ("Lift up your head, you gates, and be lifted up, you eternal doors, and the King of Glory will come in") need not obviate his subtle reference to the judge Sampson that lifted the doors of the city on his shoulders and carried them up a mountain.

(10) Take, brothers, for an example of the suffering and of the patience, the prophets who spoke in the name of the Lord. Lo, we call them blessed that endured: you have heard of the patience of Job, and have seen the end of the Lord, how that the Lord is full of pity, and merciful.

Again, his emphasis on the perfect work of patience has been a consistent theme. He dismisses failure as not a danger but as a source of joy. He dismisses the rich, proud, confident, and those who talk about faith instead of proving faith by works as double-minded. Even in what he has just stated about how the Lord operates with us, he did not use any words like propitiation, sanctification, justification, salvation, adoption, or the like: he states that the Lord is full of *pity* and *merciful*. If we do not see the solid doctrine of what he says, we have a double-minded idea of what doctrine is.

He now allows himself the luxury of a summary.

(12) But above all, my brothers, swear not, neither by the heaven, nor by the earth, nor any other oath: but let your yes be yes, and the no, no; that you fall not under judgment.

"Above all"; the desire to be *sure*, the desire to *predict*, the desire to be *right*, the desire to *be* the judge …none of these are true desires, but lusts which spring from jealousy of God himself. We are mortal; James has sketched out the path of mortals who have been given eternal life. We are mortal; we are not God, we are not judges, we are not sure of anything except that we are on a difficult path that requires us to be rich in faith and steady in patience. Failure is not a problem, trying to build ourselves a little kingdom on earth is.

The problems we encounter are not insurmountable, they are expected. The solutions to the problems can be put into a few sentences with which he closes.

(13) Is any among you suffering? let him pray. Is any cheerful? let him sing praise. Is any among you sick? let him call for the elders of the church; and let them pray over him, having anointed with oil in the name of the Lord and the prayer of the faith will save the weary one, and the Lord will raise him up; and if he have committed sins, it will be forgiven him.

And he treats our weaknesses with such grace. He does not call the sick person 'one who has erred', he calls him "the weary one". We all get weary. It is the *Lord* who raises us up. And if there *are* sins to be dealt with, no problem. "It will be forgiven him." Not '*they* will be forgiven him'; the forgiveness of sins is covered at salvation. "It" is the *fact* that he committed them, not the sins. And if there is no one standing over us ready to criticize any sins discovered (ready to "kill") we have nothing preventing us from easily confessing them and moving on.

(16) Confess therefore the offenses one to another and pray one for another, that you be healed. Very strong, the petition of a righteous one in its working.

He has opened up the avenues of help from not just the Lord, but each other. And he does not base this on some kind of assembly propriety, but on a new idea that needs properly emphasized in the path of faith: *passion*.

(17) Elijah was a man of like passions to us, and he prayed fervently that it might not rain; and it rained not on the earth for three years and six months.

(Just as a side note, I am *still* trying to figure out how James discovered that it was three years and six months. James was a man of like passions to us, and had to figure it out himself somehow.)

(18) And he prayed again; and the heaven gave rain, and the earth brought forth her fruit.

Note the parallel between praying and the proving of faith. *Both* times he prayed, and the second is described in detail. He sent his young man *seven times* to check and see if the answer was coming. We might figure that he knew it was going to rain, so no problem. Yes problem. *Someone* has to make it happen, and it is rarely easy. Daniel, when he discovered that it was time for Israel to return to the land, did not start packing his bags, he started fasting and praying, and *as a result* he got revelations about what would happen to his people long past just returning to the land.

This is one of the most beautiful endings to an epistle written. No good-byes, no telling us that Timothy is released from prison, just a straight statement about the immense difference that we can make for each other.

(19) My brothers, if any among you err from the truth, and one convert him, know that who converts a sinner from error of his way will save his soul from death, and will cover a multitude of sins.

He starts the epistle with our failures and ends the epistle with our failures; in both cases drawing out so much good that we, without his words, would have far less encouragement to persevere.

*   *   *

Thus ends James. His doctrine is unique, his method unassailable. The only option for the proud is to ignore him, which has been going on strong for nearly two thousand years. It is past the time to turn everyone's attention to his writings, it is time to turn away from those who ignore him and find fellowship with those who are "rich in faith".

Paul's Mystery
What are we doing here?

Not sure just what to say here. On pages 56 through 62 we talked about Paul's unique role and finished by mentioning that we have the key to the Mystery. While Paul says it is *revealed* in Ephesians 3:5, he does not call it a *revelation* but a "mystery".

Well then. What exactly is this Mystery?

We know that it is the mystery of God, <u>and</u> of the Father, <u>and</u> of Christ from Colossians 2:2. What about the Spirit?

We know that it is completed at the last trumpet from Revelation 10:7, First Corinthians 15:51, and First Thessalonians 4:16. What did the seven thunders say about it that John was not allowed to write down?

We know that it is connected with the assembly which is his body from Colossians 1:24-27 and Ephesians 5:30-32. How do these relate to the mystery of the seven stars in his right hand which are the seven spirits of the assemblies and the seven lamps he was amid which are the seven assemblies?

We know that it regards God's will and was hidden in God and revealed to Paul so that the full wisdom of God might be revealed to the heavenly beings through the church, from Ephesians 1:9 and 3:9-10. What does this have to do with Christ in us, the hope of glory mentioned in Colossians 1:26-27?

We know that it spans the ages and has something to do with the parable of the sower from First Corinthians 2:7, Matthew 13:11-17, Mark 4:11, and Luke 8:10. How?

We know that it has to do with blindness happening in part to Israel until the fullness of the gentiles is come in from Romans 11:25 and 16:26, and that the nations are fellow-heirs, and fellow-bodied and fellow-partakers of the promise in Christ Jesus through the gospel, from Ephesians 3:6. Partakers of what specific promise?

We know that the rulers of this age would not have crucified Jesus if they had been privy to the mystery from First Corinthians 2:7, and that it was kept silent through the times of the ages from Romans 16:25 and Ephesians 3:5. Why would not Jesus have been crucified had they known?

We know that it has to do with what godliness is from First Timothy 3:9 and 15. What new was revealed about godliness that had not been known before?

We know it is connected with the gospel from Romans 15:25 and Ephesians 6:19. How?

Ephesians 3:18 says we are to be strong to apprehend with all the saints what the breadth and length and depth and height is. Of what? And why is the up-and-down dimension given two directions: depth and height?

In fact, the more we know about the mystery, the more questions we have.

And unfortunately, theologians have universally decided that it is too difficult to figure out; so they make shortcuts like covenant theology and dispensationalism. Those are fancy terms for "We don't have the slightest idea but we're willing to argue to the death about it" This is why we took the time to look at the points in Hebrews and James. We cannot read them and hold on to our shortcuts. They make our shortcuts look a lot like shortcuts.

And it is plain to anyone who reads what scholars say regarding the book of Revelation that *no one at all* has the slightest idea what is being revealed. One of the nice things about God revealing things is that people who think that they are smarter than God are not able to understand his words, and so cannot grab them and use them to look smarter. "Wisdom is too high for a fool."

So we have something God was keeping secret. It is revealed to Paul and connects with his special gospel. It is something which the other apostles knew about, but did not emphasize, at least not using the word 'mystery' that Paul uses. This is possibly because everyone except Paul seemed to be hoping that the gospel would grow among the Jews until the nation as a whole accepted it. The fact that this was not going to happen was stated by Paul, and he *did* use the word 'mystery'. (For I would not, brothers, have you ignorant of this mystery, lest you be wise in your own conceits, that a hardening in part has befallen the Israel, until when the fullness of the nations be come in.)

But just the "fullness of the nations" needing to come in does not constitute a mystery; it was prophesied many times. We are looking for something that is *not* in prophesy.

Perhaps a good place to start would be Jesus' words on the subject from Matthew 13: "And he answering said, To you is given to know the **mysteries** of the kingdom of the heavens, but to them it is not given. For whoever has, to him will be given, and he will have abundance: but whoever has not, from him will be taken away even what he has, Therefore I speak to them in parables; because seeing they see not, and hearing they hear not, neither do they understand. And to them is fulfilled the prophecy of Isaiah, which says,

    By hearing you will hear, and in no way understand;
    And seeing you will see, and in no way perceive:
    For the heart of this people is waxed fat,
    And their ears are dull of hearing,
    And their eyes they have closed;
    Lest perhaps they should perceive with the eyes,
    And hear with the ears,
    And understand with the heart,
    And should turn again, and I should be healing them.

But blessed *your* eyes, for they see; and *your* ears, for they hear. For truly I say to you that many prophets and righteous desired to see what you see, and saw not; and to hear what you hear, and heard not. Hear *you* therefore the parable of the sower."

Now in our gospel-centric Christianity, we naturally apply the parable of the sower to giving the gospel. Plus we *moralize*; the persons who hear the gospel by the road, rocky ground, and among weeds are *bad* people, and the good ground is *good* people who listen and bear fruit.

However, anyone who has a garden knows that a path is necessary to navigate it. And there's going to be a rocky place one way or the other unless we do not bother removing rocks and throwing them somewhere. And there are going to be weeds outside the garden because the only place we remove weeds is *in* the garden where we have prepared the soil. So Jesus is giving a parable about normal conditions found in every garden. So what is the point? That we should not be so sloppy when we toss seeds?

And his next parable is about the fake wheat. Then the grain of mustard seed. Then the yeast. What on earth is Jesus saying? We take these parables and interpret them—if we bother to do so at all—according to our preferred shortcut. And arrive at the understanding of—nothing. There is nothing to be learned except some vague generalities about the kingdom of God that any simpleton could have pointed out. Birds use mustard trees. Got it. But Jesus called these the "mysteries of the kingdom of the heavens". What is so mysterious about a woman putting yeast in dough and it rising?

The disciples ask him about the parable of the fake wheat, and he explains it to them. Then he adds three: one about a treasure hidden in a field, then a merchant looking for pearls, then a net that pulls up all kinds of fish.

How do all these refer to a mystery that spans the ages and was kept secret in the Old Testament?

Later in the book he will tell a parable of the servant who would not forgive his fellow servant. Then still later he tells a series of them: the householder hiring laborers, the evil vineyard stewards, and the wedding feast no one wanted to attend.

In chapter 24 he tells them what to expect to happen in the future when they asked, after which he gives them the parable of the ten virgins with lamps, the servants trading with talents, and how he will separate sheep nations from goat nations. At this point it says he finished all these sayings. Matthew had mentioned him being finished with sayings thrice before; first when he finished commanding his disciples in 11, next when he finished "these parables" (the first seven) at the end of 13, and next when he finished "these words" (including the parable about the servant who would not forgive his fellow servant) at the beginning of 19.

This is **a lot** of talking about "the kingdom of the heavens". In fact, if we look at the whole book of Matthew which includes three solid chapters of his teaching (the 'beatitudes'), there are just over 6,000 words Jesus devotes to teaching, and well over 7,000 words he devotes to future events and the kingdom of heaven. Generally we can figure that if Jesus says something on a subject, it is something we need to hear on the subject. No wonder we are looking for shortcuts.

Stepping back and looking at all this, one element about the mystery is undeniable. It has something to do with *everyone working together within a larger construct*. The larger construct is probably going to be *larger* than the construct we try to put on it, because it says so wherever the mystery is mentioned.

We find the same element active in the Trinity arguments (for or against); two puerile assumptions are at the base of most disagreements: (1) If the persons of the Godhead are *One*, it is impossible for them to be *distinct*, and (2) If there is more than one person of the Godhead, there must be more than one God. This is the kind of logic that would say, "if melody is distinct from harmony and rhythm, it should be isolated to an entirely different kind of music." It is a special brand of shallow thinking that attempts to define by category. The trouble is, God cannot be defined, and he certainly cannot be categorized.

So we want to discover (A) What distinctions are drawn by scripture between differing elements? (B) What relationships connect these elements? and (C) What is God's larger context in which they operate together? Perhaps we can discard the artificial distinctions we have been pasting on things that have prevented us from seeing any larger context.

So we start with the parable of the sower. What we have is a *garden*. Who planted it? Does not say. Who owns it? Does not say. What determines where the path, rocky, thorny, and good ground are? It does not say, but most likely whoever made the garden. Well then what *does* it say? It says the sower sowed seed and the seeds fell into four places. He says in Luke that the seed is the word of God. In Mark it is just the word. In Matthew he says it is the word of the kingdom. In all three gospels he talks only of the condition of the ground where the seed falls. There is no opportunity for us to moralize, because each kind of ground belongs where it is. We cannot *blame* the garden pathway for being a pathway instead of being the rich soil. We cannot scold the ground that has not been tilled or weeded for having thorns. The garden owner and the sower are responsible for these things; the ground is what it is and where it is.

There is no lesson to be drawn from this parable regarding how to be good ground. We are either good ground or we are not. The thorns were already there when the seed fell among them. The seed cannot help where it fell, and the plant that grows cannot pick up and relocate to better ground. If we are looking for a way to moralize, this parable, given more space in the gospels than any other, is not a very good place to start. And this is what "many prophets and righteous" desired to hear? Why? This is the "mysteries of the kingdom of the heavens"? How?

This is not a case of them waiting for the gospel. Hebrews says "for indeed we have been evangelized even as also they; but the word of the hearing did not profit them, because they were not united by the faith with them that heard." This brings up another interesting fact: while the *disobedient* are spoken of as not "entering in" to God's rest in Hebrews four, it is apparent that *some did have the faith to enter in* such as Caleb and Joshua, for which reason the writer of Hebrews has to make the point that entering the promised land was *not* what was being referred to by the psalm. This leaves the question dangling of just where Joshua and Caleb fit in. Only two categories are mentioned: the disobedient who did not enter into God's rest, and we who do enter in. Did the writer forget something?

But this *does* establish that the 'word' that the parable speaks of was "evangelized" to Israel in the Old Testament. This broadens the scope of the parable considerably. Were Caleb and Joshua part of the "good ground" which brought forth fruit? Whatever the "word" was that they heard, it could not be identical to the gospel that we have heard, because Jesus was not yet raised from the dead. And we might have just stumbled on to one of the keys of the mystery.

Let us look at this. Where in the Old Testament was it told that the Messiah would *die* and *be raised again with a new kind of resurrection life*? There are over 300 references and quotes of the Old Testament in the New. Only three of them are used as prophetic of resurrection (Psalm 16:8-11 about not seeing corruption, Isaiah 55:3 about the sure mercies of David, and Psalm 68:18 about having ascended on high and given gifts to men). None of them when read in Old Testament context clearly prophesy resurrection. The Sadducees were politically in charge of the temple, and the main point of contention between them and the Pharisees was that they denied there was any resurrection at all, because surely if there were, the scriptures would have said so.

This is an alarming line of investigation, because we like to think that *we* know everything there is to know about resurrection, and in fact we know diddly. The subject includes the resurrection of the dead, the new bodies we are to receive, living now in resurrection life while in old bodies, how the Spirit enlivens our mortal flesh now for being able to glorify God, what will happen to those who have 'fallen asleep', who were those "saints" who Matthew says got resurrected at the same time as Jesus and what happened to them, exactly what is the 'rapture' all about, when do Old Testament saints get resurrected, who exactly composes the bride, where is the 'rapture' in Revelation; …this is a whole host of questions about which we know precisely, exactly, diddly.

This does not prevent us from making ridiculous claims about what we think we know. The trouble is that we have to make up our own construct and lay it over scripture like a filter to prove it. Dispensationalism is one of these constructs. It does not matter whether it is correct or not; what matters is that scripture does not teach it. The doctrine of the Trinity is similar: it is a construct that we put on the subject of the persons of the Godhead, of whom scripture *does* speak in very great detail, but without using our 'Trinity' construct. It does not matter whether it is correct or not; what matters is that scripture does not teach it. Why does this matter? Because the only reason we have for putting God's word into our own construct instead of using scripture's words are (1) to try to say something that scripture does not say, or (2) to make a shortcut to explain something we do not understand, or (3) both.

So let us take what we have looked at so far at face value. The sower sows the "word of the kingdom", and it is not limited to the gospel as we know it which, while telling us that we are going to inherit a kingdom, is concerned primarily with us showing faith and its works now, long before receiving a "kingdom that cannot be shaken". Jesus tells his disciples about these four kinds of ground in preparation for understanding their part in the mystery, which seems to have something do with his resurrection. The four kinds of ground *seem* to be progressive; the seed on the path gets gobbled up and never has a chance. The seed on the rocky ground springs up but withers. The seed in the thorns grows but gets choked and does not bear fruit. The seed on the good ground bears fruit but in differing amounts. He is answering a question that had been plaguing prophets from the beginning. But what is it?

While we are talking about 'kinds of ground' what about Hebrews six where it talks about ground that bears "thorns and thistles, it is disapproved and near a curse; whose end is to be burned"? It looks like the writer of Hebrews adds a whole new category of ground.

In the parable of the fake wheat (which he also explains) the seed is not the "word of the kingdom" but "the sons of the kingdom". This parable satisfies the need for the useless to be removed. But we get no such 'gathering' or 'casting into the furnace of fire' in the first parable. In fact, there is nothing whatsoever said about what becomes of those that do not bear fruit. If it *says* nothing about what we call 'salvation', then quite possibly it is not about salvation. What is it about?

Well, it would have to be about bearing fruit.

When we went through James, we noticed that he says "the fruit of righteousness in peace is sown to them that make peace". We connected this through Proverbs to the tree of life, but we did not explore the subject very far; only to note that those who make peace are providing the ground in which grows the tree of life. If we are looking for something that spans the ages, the tree of life seems like a good place to start.

So now we have three places to start: the tree of life, resurrection life, and the parable of the sower… each of which by itself is completely inexplicable. What if they are all talking about the same thing?

Even though God breathed into Adam the "breath of life" and he became a "living soul", he still had to be prevented from eating of the "tree of life" once he ate of the tree of the knowledge of good and evil. What is different about the life that the tree of life has? When God said, "lest he stretch out his hand, and take of the tree of life, and live forever..." we take it that this means live forever in these bodies with blood in them that "cannot inherit the kingdom of God", thus shutting us out from his kingdom. So the very existence of the "tree of life" implies an entirely different kind of life that had become inappropriate to have in these bodies.

Some realization of this fact was operative in humans. Hebrews says "These all died according to faith, not having received the promises, but having seen them and greeted from afar, and having confessed that they were strangers and pilgrims on the earth. For who say such things manifest that they are seeking after a country of their own. And if indeed they had minded that from which they went out, they would have had opportunity to return. But now they desire a better, that is, a heavenly: for which reason the God is not ashamed of them, to be called their God; for he has prepared them a city." They did this "**not** accepting the deliverance, that they might obtain a better resurrection", and "received not the promise, the God having foreseen something better concerning us, that apart from us they be not made perfect."

We touched on this last phrase when we went through Hebrews, but isolated our comments to how it justifies God. It is evident that what is being talked about is *not* 'going to heaven', an idea that in the middle ages transformed what was to be a life of hope and patience into a life of hopelessness and apprehension. In Protestantism this was further transformed by Evangelicalism into getting as many people into heaven for their eternal security as possible and assessing a church's worth by a straight tally of the results. The veracity of this approach was never questioned by either camp, and as a result we have little to no idea what we are doing on earth in the interim.

If there is an entirely different kind of life available—to be lived now—that on the one hand makes us "pilgrims and strangers" but on the other hand allow us to 'subdue kingdoms', 'stop lions' mouths', 'turn to flight armies of aliens', and 'receive our dead by resurrection', then the question of 'going to heaven' seems to be comparatively moot.

If this new and different kind of life was available *by faith* to humans even before Jesus, then what we have received in having knowledge of a "mystery" was operative then, as now, and is a continuation of that process aided by events that have allowed what was previously a secret to be exposed. The path has not changed; we are simply at a point further along on the same path that Abel was on. And the God who translated Enoch so that he did not see death does that kind of thing any time he wants, to anyone he wants. This path is described in great detail in Job 28 as the path to Wisdom, contrasted with earthly wisdom, appropriately depicted as mining.

Meanwhile this path has always had the elusive tree of life—and by proxy our expectation to have access to it—planted in the garden of God way back in the beginning before man existed. And when we read Revelation, at the end of the path also.

So it appears that our very definition of the word 'resurrection' is tainted by a middle ages idea of going to heaven, obscuring the fact that it is a kind of life that we are to be operating in now, just as Sampson did in his day. If this is so, we could expect some light on how this 'tree of life' is used in a practical way by humans still in flesh and blood. Proverbs is the only book beside Genesis and Revelation that talks of the tree of life; the first time in relation to living with Wisdom: "She is tree of life to ones holding fast in her, and those upholding her are made happy."

Well "holding fast" sounds a lot like a solution to the birds of the air 'snatching away' the word of the kingdom from those of us that find ourselves traveling on the road instead of settled into good ground. When we are not somewhere we can bear fruit, as the seed which fell on the path or the case in the church of Philadelphia, we can at least "hold fast".

Next in Proverbs we get "Fruit of righteous—tree of life. And taking souls—wise." This "taking" is first used when God 'took' the rib from Adam to build the woman. It is appropriate, when nothing further can be done in the circumstances; for example, if there is no depth of root, to gather the souls to where something useful can be done with them, where "fruit of righteousness" can be produced *in them* since it cannot be produced *by them*. It took the peace-makers—those who prepare the ground—until

Abraham before enough depth of soil existed for faith to take root. Hebrews gives as examples of this preparation the *witness* of Abel and the *godly fear* of Noah.

Third in Proverbs, "Hope deferred, making ill heart. And tree of life—desire comes." Many translations say 'desire fulfilled is a tree of life' which is a similar idea. This is what we saw in James regarding not knowing how to desire, and spending our efforts on lust instead. If there is patience in our hope, we will not see it as deferred. If we are in a place on the path that is not properly prepared for the hope we want to see implemented *right now* (as Solomon building the house of God but not realizing that the true house of God would be built of living stones; people), we will allow our heart to grow ill, and get "choked" by the cares of this world and the deceitfulness of riches, as did he.

Lastly in Proverbs we have "Healing of tongue, tree of life. And subversion in her—breaking in spirit." This brings us to the "good ground" and makes sense of James' spending so much time on the issue at stake now: the tongue. The woman of worth is praised at the end of Proverbs for having the "law of kindness" under her tongue.

What we are seeing here is a constant dynamic interaction in all ages of—propitiation: Christ interceding to make things work regardless of the circumstances. When the cherubim was placed between Adam and the tree of life, it was just like the veil placed between the people and the holy of holies. Jesus took on a human body that *became* the veil; he stepped into the picture and embodied the dividing element, then allowed that embodiment to die, eliminating the division and making peace. This is one of the many ways he *stepped in*. In fact, he has 'stepped' in to such an extent that it now appears that *we* are the foreign element and he is the true human. Which, as it turns out, has always been the case.

It is difficult to speak of such things when the audience does not have the experience of considering them. It is inappropriate to prop up the indolent with nice words. It is useful, however, to remind those who have been long struggling in circumstances outside of their control that Christ has been doing so for far longer, and that we are working together. But doctrines and theories about doctrines, apart from Jesus, make the soul sick.

So the tree of life tells us of a new kind of life that we did not receive from the "breath of life" or becoming a "living soul". The path to that tree of life is the path of Wisdom. The companion on that path is the Spirit of Christ. The energy that faith can access on that path is resurrection life, which is the subject of the Mystery. It was not revealed until Jesus was resurrected because (1) the ground was not prepared to produce the fruit of righteousness, because it is the Spirit who is the gardener and produces the fruits of the Spirit in us, and he could not physically come until Jesus physically received resurrection life, and (2) those who wish to "force" their way into the kingdom of God would have tried to abrogate this resurrection life, or prevent it altogether. "The law and the prophets until John: from that time the glad tidings of the kingdom of the God are announced, and every one forces his way into it."

Jesus went through a lot of trouble to make sure he was crucified when and how he was. The leaders had already determined that it was not to be during the Passover; Jesus had different plans. Satan, the Romans, the Jews, everyone joined together to do exactly what Jesus and God wanted them to do. When the resurrection occurred, there was a stunned "Oops" across the spiritual and physical realms. They played right into his hands. Had they known what resurrection life actually was, they would never have participated. God got all those who hate him to do his work for him. And Jesus saw to it that it was done exactly how he wanted it done.

We do not find this aspect of Christ's work emphasized because many of us like to have a poor helpless victim Jesus whom we can pity and emulate by acting pitiful. This makes for great religion because it looks holy to be pitiful. This is called false humility. The man who faced down the entire Sanhedrin and Pilate did not back down one inch. And the fact that he did not resist alarmed them and incited them to try harder to get a reaction out of him. All they got was "If I have spoken evil, witness of the evil: but if well, why do you smite me?"

Nor does anyone want to seem to emphasize the quote from Isaiah found in *all four gospels*, *as well as* the summary of Acts:
> By hearing you will hear, and in no way understand;
> And seeing you will see, and in no way perceive:
> For the heart of this the people is waxed fat,
> And their ears are dull of hearing,
> And their eyes they have closed;
> Lest perhaps they should perceive with the eyes,
> And hear with the ears,
> And understand with the heart,
> And should turn again, and I should be healing them.

God was tired of Israel taking advantage of the fact that he always bailed them out. He essentially sent Jesus saying, 'Okay, give them the word, but give it to them in such a way that they will not listen. I am done with them.' While, yes, Jesus came to address the sin of the world, he also came to *make certain* that Israel rejected him and thus removed themselves from muddling up the mystery by saying that they owned the rights to it. This happened in specific stages, the whole of which, in legal detail, are laid out in Isaiah as well as the other prophets, which show us what exactly was happening in the book of Acts. When preparing the ground for the tree of life to grow, the last thing you need is a bunch of people helping who want to plant the tree of the knowledge of good and evil instead.

Adam had invested the hope that the *very existence* of the tree of life offered, into his wife. It was his last recorded word. "And Man called his wife's name Eve; because she is the mother of all living." It was in this spirit that Jesus says the kingdom of heaven is like a woman who hid yeast in three measures of meal. The yeast is the hope of the kingdom; the meal is the unprepared hearts of humanity; she "hid" it because those who take the kingdom of God by force would attempt to steal and kill for it; she had seen what her own son did to Abel.

It takes time and patience for us to grow: thousands of years at last count. Meanwhile we need preserved. And while we are being preserved for better things to come, we need good things right now or we lose heart. Now that the knowledge of the resurrection is known, new fruit can be produced that was not produced before. Before the resurrection, Sampson could be criticized as indiscreet with women. After the resurrection and Christ passing through the heavenlies, no one (with any spiritual sense) dares criticize him, because he is now "in Christ" and only God is judge. We do not include here those who can do nothing *except* moralize and judge.

And so the good ground is secured; we are rooted and grounded, so as to be strong to apprehend with all the saints what is the breadth and length and depth and height. This is of the realm in which resurrection life is normal. The breadth and length and height refer to the dimensions of the New Jerusalem, all equal, and the depth refers to the riches of the wisdom and knowledge of 'God who builds all things'. The house of God is built on the *foundation* of the apostles and prophets, Jesus Christ himself being the cornerstone, and we will not take the time here to sketch out the relationship between this house and the city, save that one is mother of us all, and the other is all of us.

This introduces the first element of the mystery; that it could not be revealed until its time although it was the plan all along. But merely knowing that it has to do with the word of the kingdom and with resurrection life (shown in planting the tree of life) is only the beginning; these are only the stepping stones into the mystery. We can partly see now why it is called the mystery of God and of the Father, and of Christ, but not 'of' the Spirit because it was prepared *for* the Spirit to operate in. Jesus said "My father works even until now and I work", and "this is the work of God, that you believe on him whom *he* has sent." But we look in vain for any scripture connecting any 'work' with the Spirit.

We can see that it is not completed yet, because the patience of the saints is not completed yet. This is the patience that is the theme of the book of James. This patience is the first quality listed of love itself in First Corinthians 13, and is called the patience of the Christ in Second Thessalonians 3. John introduces himself in Revelation as "fellow-partaker in the tribulation and kingdom and patience in Jesus". God has determined a last trumpet to herald the occasion of the proving of our faith working patience so that patience itself perfects its own work, that we be perfect and entire. God has indicated that nothing will hold back resurrection life once this trumpet sounds; even our bodies will be transformed. The details of these events cannot be understood without being a participant in "the patience and the faith of the saints". The seven thunders for which we *do* have records teach us this: The first is when dividing the waters in on the second day, described in Psalm 104. The next two are in Exodus, to show God's power first to his enemies then to his people. The next two are in First Samuel, first to protect his people then to chastise them. The sixth thunder is in the establishing of David over his kingdom described in Psalms 18 and 29; and the seventh to judge his kingdom in Isaiah 29. The seven thunders sketch out God's dealings with the earth, his people, and his kingdom, and have a message from them that John was told not to write down, forcing us to search it out for ourselves.

We can see that the true temple could be begun once the ground that was prepared for the seed was available. Jesus said, Destroy this temple, and in three days I will raise it up, speaking of the temple of his body, and Paul elaborates "Know you not that you are God's temple, and the Spirit of the God dwells in you?" This building could not be *physically* started (and it is rather useful to know what applies to the physical and how) until a *physical* man with a *physical* body" passed through the heavens". Paul later uses this *same truth* about being the temple of the Holy Spirit, not collectively like he did in First Corinthians three above, but individually to their bodies in chapter six to address the subject of fornication. That is rather physical. We have precise instructions regarding the protocols between the physical and spiritual realities that we encounter; as well as how and why they relate.

This operating physically together is the subject of the 'church' or 'assembly'. *Lots* of words are given to it by all the writers.

"The assembly which is his body" is a physical fact. The phrase 'the mystical body of Christ' is used a lot because people *need* it to be mystical instead of physical even though a 'body' is about as synonymous with 'physical' as meaning allows. So the "assembly" or 'church' is the physical gathering of living humans who are being built into a holy temple, God's house, in spirit. ...What? Which; 'physical' or 'in spirit'? Well both; we do have both a spirit and a body. The assembly is physical. Our body is physical. The physical body we have is not the 'spiritual body' (a strange expression) that we will have when resurrection life is completed in us. When the "marriage of the Lamb is come," it will be when "his wife has made herself ready." This will *not* be in these bodies we have now, if we are counted among those who have part in her. Just as 'corruption cannot inherit incorruption', the current "body of Christ", while being the "assembly of Living God, pillar and ground of the truth", is also a "great house" in which are vessels to honor and dishonor alike. The physical aspect is right now. The local 'church' is to be treated with the full dignity of Christ's body because *he* does so. We can get a good idea of what he allows and what he rejects —and when—from his messages to angels of the seven churches in Revelation. He puts up with a lot.

There is, however, no local 'house of God' and no local 'temple'. These are spiritual. This does not mean that we do not interact with them physically. When Paul refers to us being the temple, both collectively and individually, the physical consequences are stated: "If any corrupts the temple of the God, him will the God corrupt; for the temple of God is holy, which you are." This allows God to distinguish (in this strange interim in which we have resurrection life in physical bodies) between the vessels of honor and the vessels of dishonor. This also allows him to decide who is the wheat and who is the fake wheat. We would very much like to be in charge of deciding that. We are not. Not for our own bodies, not in our churches, and not with each other. The only judging a church is instructed to act on is in response to outward actions, not states of heart. If we even try to analyze our own hearts as to how much we truly love God and how much we are fooling ourselves, we will either end up insane or have to make up a whole bunch of non-biblical creeds to support our inanity. We are neither called nor competent to judge God's judgment on ourselves.

So the mystery Jesus explained to John in Revelation of the seven stars in his right hand, which are the seven spirits of the assemblies, and the seven lamps he was amid, which are the seven assemblies, really is a mystery; it is how he is operating with very physical people who have been brought into a very spiritual realm. We are learning, not that resurrection life means we are going to heaven, but that resurrection life is an entirely different kind of living right now.

All kinds of new experiences come in and we need new ways to handle them. Paul writes to Timothy, "that you know how one is to behave in God's house, the which is assembly of Living God, pillar and ground of the truth. And admittedly, great is the mystery of the godliness;
>   Who was manifested in flesh,
>   Justified in spirit,
>   Seen of angels,
>   Preached among nations,
>   Believed on in world,
>   Received up in glory.

This is part of the mystery; How do we act? What is 'godliness' now like? There are two parts of the mystery that Paul calls 'great': the relationship between a man and a woman as applied to Christ and the church, and godliness. The first we may go into; for now let us look at what he says about godliness.

There are three pairs of statements that are set in contrast regarding the Author and Finisher of our faith. He was manifest in *flesh*, but justified in *spirit*. He was seen of *angels* but preached among *nations*. He was believed on in *world*, but received up in *glory*. The initial lessons for us are straightforward. We find ourselves in a body, but what we do every day—how hard we work to be godly—does not justify us; rather we need justified in s*pirit*; that is, the things that we do have to address a spiritual reality *before* they can properly address the physical reality. Next Jesus was seen of angels but preached among nations; this is a complete reversal. God and the angels see what we do, and God may very well approve of what we do; but for godliness to be efficacious, *people have to be so impressed with our actions that they notice*. False humility would have us hide our lamp under a bushel basket. Lastly he was believed on in world, but received up in glory. Another complete reversal. If people are noticing what we do and accept it as good, the worst thing we can do is be received into their society or received into their houses. Jesus said of those who accept this kind of honor, "they *have* their reward". There is enough of God's work for us to fill several lifetimes (unless we happen to be competent like Jesus), the time for reception and honor is when we are done.

And it is that simple.

John says "even as *he* is, *we* also are in this world." Remember that resurrection life was "hid in God"—this means that the angels were unaware of it… and certainly the "rulers of this world" including Satan were unaware of it. Resurrection life is not something the angels say 'Ho hum, old hat stuff' to. And it was introduced to *humans* of all creatures, meaning that angels are, in fact, quite interested in learning what it is all about. Paul says we are engaged in "the fellowship of the mystery" which was brought to light "that now unto the principalities and the powers in the heavenlies be made known through the church the manifold wisdom of the God, according to a plan of the ages which he made in the Christ Jesus our Lord." It is so connected with what Christ is doing *now*—we being the body and he being the head—that Paul says in Colossians that the mystery "is Christ in you, the hope of the glory".

This brings us to what the short-cutters say that the 'mystery' is. It is difficult to summarize all the shortcuts since there seems to be one for every nuance of opinion, but most quote Ephesians 3 for an attempt at a definition: "that the nations are fellow-heirs, and fellow-bodied and fellow-partakers of the promise in Christ Jesus through the gospel". It *is* a mouthful, but hardly a *definition* because one is expected to know what he is talking about. *What is this promise?* It goes beyond the promise to Abraham or Moses; Hebrews points out that the eternal covenant is based on "better promises". Paul claimed that God had promised the resurrection of Jesus all along when speaking to the Jews in Acts 13, though his identification of how God had done so was quite new to his audience. We *have* received the "promise of my Father", the Holy Spirit, which Peter reiterates at the end of Acts two. As for future, James refers to "the crown of life" as well as the "kingdom" as our current promises.

But the gospel is only the *means* of accessing the "promise in Christ Jesus". Paul refers to it when writing to Timothy the second time as the "promise of life". *Fortunately* we have the maverick John to chip in, and he says plainly, "And this is the promise which he promises us: the life, the eternal."

Hm. Eternal life. Is that anything like resurrection life? That would mean we would have to discard our Middle Ages idea that eternal life means living forever and accept it for what it is: "and this is the eternal life, to know you, the only true God, and whom you did send." At this point it is overwhelmingly evident that the 'mystery' is not one-dimensional. If "the nations are fellow-heirs, and fellow-bodied and fellow-partakers of the promise" of "the life, the eternal", which is "in Christ Jesus", how are we to understand all the issues—specifically the physical order and timing—surrounding resurrection? We did mention a few paragraphs back that our knowledge of these issues is roughly diddly, give or take some posturing.

This takes us back to the parables. In Matthew Jesus tells no less than fourteen parables on the subject of the kingdom. He also gives them a long explanation of what to actually expect, and in what order. We would really like to be able to make sense of it all somehow. The problem is that we lack the witness of Jesus, "for the witness of Jesus is the spirit of the prophecy." The disciples did *not* have our problem; he asked them, "Have you understood all these? They say to him, Yes. And he said to them, Therefore every scribe discipled to the kingdom of the heavens is like a man, a householder, who brings forth out of his treasure new and old." So the understanding applies both to the new and old 'testaments'. There is a distinction between the new and old treasures, and there are common elements that tie them together, both of which require us to be *scribes* discipled to the kingdom of the heavens.

Being a scribe takes diligent attention to scripture using a tradition of tools competent in "cutting in a straight line the word of truth". This can be difficult to do when the cutting tool we have been handed is a spoon, and the tradition available to us is obfuscation. Jesus had to tell the scribes of his day that they were completely ignoring the "weightier matters of the law" and these were considered the most highly educated in the world at interpreting scripture. They were overly concerned with *What should we do?* We get overly concerned with *What is the answer?* Yes, we need answers. But the issues with which we are to be occupied do not concern answers to questions but building a temple. A building block can be analyzed for years; at some point it needs to be put into the building.

So what is a scribe to do? Read what it says. Scripture is rather precise about how to interpret scripture. We could go into types, antitypes, archetypes, promises, covenants, hopes, prophecies, and many more scribal tools, but the purpose of this paper is to sketch out Paul's mystery, not interpret the entirety of scripture. So let us summarize.

The mystery concerns what was hidden until Jesus was resurrected. It includes the covenants and promises, all of them. It gives the scope of what God counseled for the earth, humanity, and more precisely, for Christ before the ages of time. What little we know of it gives us a glimpse into eternal matters to which mankind is a relative newcomer. As for its effect to us today, it shows specifically how God is able to open the way of life to all people in all times, not just his chosen people or the Christians. It tells us what we are doing right now and who is watching for what reason. It informs us as to true godliness, the relationship between a husband and a wife (which we did not go into), our relationship to the angels and other beings, the way God handles Israel, the way Christ handles the church, the role of the Spirit, the relationship between eternal life and resurrection life, the place of the tree of life, the protocols of the kingdom of God, and how to operate in the kingdom of God *now* before it is fully implemented.

All this (for us) is "to know the love of the Christ which passes the knowledge, that you be filled unto all the fullness of the God". This is the reason it is called a mystery. It is past knowledge, just as "the peace of God, which surpasses every understanding, will guard your hearts and your thoughts by Christ Jesus." The fact that it is past knowledge does not mean that we cannot know it, it means that there is more to know in its full scope than we can take.

Afterword

It is time for the torch to be passed from Christianity to what is next. It has been a long journey, and once the blindfolds are removed and the eye-salve applied, we will probably be pleasantly surprised to find out what has really been happening all this time.

The fellowship "with the Father and with his Son Jesus Christ" was a refreshing change for this age. There is quite a bit of difference between expecting a messiah and finding out that he is someone we can begin to know, who knows us. He revealed the Father as 'Dad' (Abba) and introduced the Spirit as the "Comforter". It made quite a change in our growth process.

Paul got himself a visit to the third heaven, and managed to put some of it into words, for which, of course, he got himself locked away. But the words of the apostles have come down to us in a form still effective despite our tendency to make idols. The untold story of how the temple has been being built over these centuries, when told, will easily replace our distractions with non-issues. "But many first will be last, and last first."

The actual torch we have to pass along is not doctrinal. "By this will all know that you are my disciples, if you have love one to another." The world is doing, and will continue to do, everything it can to prevent life. As hard as it is for us to believe, they really do want to "destroy the earth". Fortunately for us, this is not a battle that we need to engage in: "be of good courage: I have overcome the world." "Here is the patience and the faith of the saints." To those who pick up the fallen mantle after us we say, Welcome to the fellowship, and welcome to the household of God.